CONDITIONAL FREE ECONOMY & CONDITIONAL DEMOCRACY

Misapplication of Economics Theory

2016年9月6日

HIROSHI MORITA
Tokyo, Japan

Conditional Free Economy
&
Conditional Democracy.

Hands-on Economics Theory.

Misapplication of economics theory on the fundamentally changed world.

Copyright © 2016 Hiroshi Morita all rights reserved.

First Edition (September, 2016)

Contents:

目次

Business Style Summary

Preface

Overview

Background

Introduction

Body

    Chapter 1. Starting from Adam Smith

    Chapter 2. Consumption Driven Economy

    Chapter 3. Case Study: Financial crisis in 2007-2008

    Chapter 4. Dysfunctional economics theory

    Chapter 5: Going back to basics

    Chapter 6. Adam Smith's Teachings

    Chapter 7. Monopoly

    Chapter 8. Deregulations

    Chapter 9 TPP

    Chapter 10. Symptoms V.S. A Real Cause

    Chapter 11. A New Business Model

    Chapter 12. Conditional Free Economy and Conditional Democracy

    Chapter 13. Economic Gains

    Chapter 14. Change of our Life Styles

    Chapter 15. A New Economics Model

    Chapter 16. Dysfunctional U.S. Economy

    Chapter 17. Change Economic System

    Chapter 18. Additional Information

    Chapter 19. Industry Driven Economy

    Chapter 20. Population Management

    Chapter 21. Impact of the Climate Change

    Chapter 22. Summaries

Conclusion

Bibliography

About the Author

Business Style Summary:

I. Problem ID:
   A. Saturation of the Earth with about 7.3 billion human beings those who emit CO_2 and use up natural resources. According to Mr. Richard Branson, affordable population on the earth is estimated about 5 billion by scientists. This is equivalent to having too many fishes in a small pond situation, where there is not enough room for growth left anymore. (118 years of reserve for coal, for example.) We have no control over population growth so far.
   B. Still using the growth or expansion model for economics and business on the contrary that there is not much room left for growth. Consumption driven economy is also triggering population growth by improving subsistence according to my learnings and analysis. Since our situation has been already changed, the current growth model is already unfit. (No growth model such as CIRCULAR ECONOMY of Ms. Ellen MacArthur must be more appropriate from now on.) As economy grows, population will grow inevitably because of increased subsistence.
   C. Co-existence of free economy and Chinese controlled economy is causing dysfunction of self-adjusting mechanism or invisible hand because fundamental assumptions of free economy such as free flow of exchange rate, for example, is being violated by Chinese government right now. (Conditional free economy may be more appropriate right now. In Rome, do as Romans do.)

II. Current Situations:
We are now facing with the Climate Change and thus we need to change/adjust ourselves accordingly. In other words, we need to change everything such as our economic and business systems as well as our life styles, habits, and behaviors altogether in accordance with each other.

According to Dawning theory, "those who survives are not the smartest nor the strongest but be responsive. ("Poor Charlie's Almanack", Charles T. Munger.)

III. Issues:
We are killing ourselves in a most efficient and quick way by using growth/expansion models for both economy and business while also knowing that there exist visible limitations in front of us. Resources are getting scarce and room for expansion is getting very limited. Therefore, our economic and business theories contradict to our realities. We need to either adjust our theories accordingly or apply theory more cautiously and appropriately.

IV. Alternatives:
1. Status Quo. Kill ourselves as quickly and efficiently as possible.
2. Go for CIRCULAR ECONOMY proposed by Ms. Ellen MacArthur
3. Apply Conditional free economy and Conditional Democracy in a transitional period.

V. Recommendation:
I personally recommend (3), which is applying conditional free economy and conditional democracy for the time being since the implementation of CIRCULAR ECONOMY will require us drastic changes and it will be very hard for us to implement it right away. Besides, Adam Smith persistently recommends that any change should be "gradual" based on his logics.

Preface

Purpose of this book:

Purpose of this book is to share with you what I learned and analyzed and thus make you re-aware of our future choices so that we will not end up unconsciously taking the path which may lead us not the best outcome when taking all factors into considerations.

<Environmental Change>

(We have to change ourselves accordingly.)

Since our environment has been changed and will be changed further in the future, we need to adjust to it accordingly. What does it mean to us? We need to change almost everything such as our life styles, business systems, and economic system, etc., also. We need to change them all at once in accordance with each other "gradually".

<Causes>

1. Overpopulation.

Human beings have used up natural resources to the extent that those are no longer abundant such as fossil fuels, which consequently triggered and having caused environmental changes, namely global warming. In other words, it is very clear that our economic activities have caused global warming since only human beings use fossil fuels on earth. None of the other animals never use fossil fuels.

<Balance>

(Economic prosperity V.S. Survival.)

Now we have a challenge to face. We need to find out a balance between the two, our survival and economic prosperity.

Up until now after the World War II, we have only pursued economic prosperity based on economic growth model aiming for expansion and maximizing consumptions, which is consumption driven economy.

Since our environment has been changed, this kind of economic model/system is completely unfit and no longer appropriate nor justifiable.

<So what do we need to do?>

We need to see and act from a bird-eye point of view instead of just narrowly focused economic point of view. We need to stop acting like a king of animal kingdom. According to evolutionary theory, life or a living cell has been born from the Nature. Human beings have been born from the Nature. The Nature is a mother/master and human beings belong to it. Destroying the Nature means killing ourselves. We are just borrowing earth for our living and thus we need to use it clan and keep it clean.

Since our environment has been changed and will be changed drastically based on our educated guess, I would like to share with you what I learned and found out in order to be better fitted for the changed environment and further changing environments.

According to Dawning theory, "those who survives are not the smartest nor the strongest but be responsive. ("Poor Charlie's Almanack", Charles T. Munger.)

You see, we have to respond to the change!

Conclusion:

<Change Economic System>

(From Expansion/growth model to Non growth model in the end.)

Switch from our current free economy to CIRCULAR ECONOMY (Ms. Ellen MacArthur) is recommended in the end.

As a transit process, conditional free economy is recommended since we need to slow down our economy before stopping. (Conditional means that it is free on the condition that it does not hurts the public interests. In other words, some restrictions will be imposed instead of completely free.)

While writing this book, I saw Ms. Ellen MacArthur's presentation in "TED" on TV about CIRCULAR ECONOMY, I thought that "this is it." However, I also noticed the difficulty of its implementation. How can we go from free economy to CIRCULAR ECONOMY all of a sudden? These two economies are heading toward 180 degree opposite direction and thus we need a transitory process. Conditional economy can be used for this purpose because it is just a slight modification of free economy.

Actual Work:

First I thought that this is none of my business since I am not an economist nor a person in power. Secondly, I was afraid of being criticized by economists because actually I am not sufficiently qualified for this. I tried to qualify myself mostly by my self-education, though. I taught myself by reading Adam Smith's book three times in a row. I do not even have a master degree in economics but I did take both microeconomics and macroeconomics classes of graduate level as mandatory requirements for my MBA at UCR. I may lose more than I will get by being attacked by qualified economists with Ph.D. if I talk about Economics per se. It means that in business terms "leave junks to somebody else." In free economy, if everybody minds his/her own business, everything will be fine because of self-adjusting mechanism of invisible hand works, right? Not really. Self-adjusting mechanism of invisible hand is not working properly right now based on our past observations and experiences so far. In other words, our economy is not working properly as it is intended by the economics theory right now. Why? Because we are violating basic assumptions of economics theory right now. What does it mean? We are violating the use instructions. So what should we do? We have to do something about it right now very quickly before it is too late. If nobody is doing it, I have to do it; that is my conclusion.

Here I am trying to update Adam Smith's "the Wealth of Nations", which is next to impossible for me obviously and thus I will just talk about application of economic theory instead of theory itself.

By the way, I got this idea when I read a sentence such that "somebody have to update Adam Smith's wealth of nations since …" in Dr. Laurence C. Smith's book titled "The world in 2050." Do you know that I thought at that time? Obviously I am not qualified. This is not my job since my major is not economics and thus most likely some economists or some Ph.D. will attack me if I do. It is their job. After a while, I pondered why nobody is doing? Obviously I do not have an answer for it. Everybody is minding his/her own business, I guess, which is perfectly fine based on the concept of free economy. But I questioned myself how can I do it? Then I noticed that if I mainly talk about application of economics theory instead of theory itself, it should be fine. Qualifications do not matter to me when our situations are getting worse in spite of economists or experts' alleviation of symptoms. Also if nobody is doing it, I have to do it from an urge deep inside in me. Therefore, this is just getting your attention and reminding you that we have to do something about it fundamentally ASAP before it's too late.

Overview:

1. Changed environment -> Change system:
   Since environment has been changed, we need to change our system accordingly. Since a drastic environmental change is predicted due mainly to the Climate Change, we may need to change our system drastically from now on.

2. Economics theory and its implementation:
   "Economics theory only works under certain conditions or in a narrow range" according to Dr. Auerbach, an economics professor in 1986 at GSM, UCR. According to my understanding, this also means that economics theory will not work when it does not meet requirements or basic assumptions, which is happening right now.
   For example, laissez faire only works well under no limitation. When there exit severe limitations such as the situation right now, laissez faire is not the best option obviously. This is self-evident if we use our logics. When we do not have enough foods, it is best for us to share foods together. If we leave it to laissez faire, some of us get more than enough and thus lots of us may go starvation, for example.
   There are assumptions to meet because economics theory is basically based on mathematics and logics. If we do not meet these assumptions, economics theory does not work as promised or an invisible hand does not work properly, which is the case right now.
   In this case, we need to run simulations on every economics theory based on what if scenarios one by one such as follows:
   a. What if oil is running out in 30 years?
   b. What if coal is running out in 118 years?
   c. Etc.
      In other words, we are imposing limitations one by one as opposed to no limitation scenario.

   1. <Example of Consumption driven economy.>

Consumption driven economy is the best on the condition that there exist no limitations, right?

What will happen when oil is running out in 30 years? This creates a limitation. We want to save oil as long as possible in this case. Don't you think so? Do we want to spend or use up oil as quickly and efficiently as possible? No! However, we are actually using up oil as quickly and efficiently as possible by using consumption driven economy. Consumption driven economy is the worst choice for the purpose of saving oil, for example. In other words, we can no longer afford consumption driven economy when considering for saving oil.

Can you see it as follows?

<Diagnosis>
1. When no limitations: Consumption driven economy may be the best.
2. With a limitation of oil: Consumption driven economy must be the worst.

Therefore, optimal point or equilibrium must be in-between depending on how desperately we need to save oil.

In conclusion, Diagnosis first and application second.

Right now, we are blindly applying economics theory without any diagnosis of the market condition whether it is healthy, normal, and applicable or not.

<Reasons: Violation of basic assumptions.>

Free economy is not theoretically compatible with controlled economy such as that of China. Self-adjusting mechanism or an invisible hand will not work when exchange rate is fixed or controlled within a certain range by Chinese government, for example. In free economy, "natural and free state" is an assumption. Basic assumptions of free economy includes free flow of exchange rate and right now this assumption is violated by Chinese government, namely by controlling or manipulating. That is most likely why the trade balance between the U.S. and China is not self-adjusting right now if I am not mistaken.

3. Free economy only works properly in peace and healthy conditions:

<Free economy, no intervention = no medication.>
<Diagnosis first and application next.>
<Healthy or unhealthy?>

This is the same with an analogy of human body mechanism. As long as we are healthy, we do not need to take any medicines since we have self-healing mechanisms in our body. Opposite is also true. If we take medicines when we are healthy, it is only harmful instead of beneficial/helpful since they only give us side effects and thus we will be worse off.

Therefore, we need to take medicines when it is absolutely necessary or when we are sick.

By the same token, Adam Smith recommends no medicine or no intervention, which is free economy since self-adjusting mechanism will work. (This only apply or true in peace and healthy conditions.)

A. As long as we are healthy, we do not need to take any medicines.
   When healthy, free economy.
B. When we are sick, we need to take medications.
   When unhealthy, non-free economy = some interventions, regulations.

   When we get sick, it may be better off to take medicines given that effective medicines are available.

   In Adam Smith's era, there weren't effective medicines available as far as I know. This may be why Adam Smith recommends taking no medicine, which is equivalent to free economy (laissez-faire), and rely on self-adjusting mechanism of free economy. This is basically the same as self-healing mechanism of human body in healthy conditions in my opinion.
   By the way, in Adam Smith's era in around 1776, basically no effective medicine were available. Effective medicines are found and became usable/available about 150 years later than Adam Smith's era. Penicillin, the first anti-biotics, was discovered by Fleming in 1929 and it became available during the World War II. Lots of wounded soldiers died of wounds/cuts because of infections developed thereafter. In other words, people of Adam Smith's era lived without effective medicines such as anti-biotics.

BY the same token, regulations were primitive in Adam Smith's era and people at that time had not accumulated enough knowledges and data about how regulations affect economies and thus regulations often times made matters worse in Adam Smith's era inferring from his book.

On the contrary, we now have effective medicines. We also have enough experiences and knowledge for handling regulations and thus we will be better off applying regulations properly on necessary basis. (On the condition that when economy is unhealthy such as monopoly/oligopoly condition exists, etc.)

4. Democracy only works properly in peace and healthy conditions.
   <Diagnosis first and application next.>
   When war situation or emergency situation, military system works better than democracy because it takes too long to implement or get things done quickly enough under democracy system.
   For example, Dr. Ben Carson, M.D. said in his commencement talk that (US national debt)" we are living in a country right now has a seventeen-and a-half trillion-dollar national debt. ...if you tried to pay it back, at a rate of ten million dollars a day,... it would take you forty-seven hundred years to pay that back." (Regent University, class of 2014, "Remembering Who We Are")
   Who can survive for 4700 years? Why is that? Because it is democracy.
   Do you know coal will be running out in about 118 years from now?
   Democracy only works well in peace and healthy conditions. At emergency condition, military system works better. Right now, we are in semi-emergency situation in my opinion, conditional democracy is more appropriate in my opinion. (Democracy is great on the condition that it does not hurt the public interests.)
   In other words, democracy will not work properly when war, emergency, and unhealthy conditions.
   People think and act illogically when unhealthy, emergency, and war conditions.
   Therefore, Conditional democracy is recommended when conditions are not healthy.

   (Conditional Democracy when unhealthy conditions.)

Conditional democracy is in between democracy and military system. Under the democracy, everything is bottom up. On the other hands, in military system, commands are top down. In conditional democracy, most things are bottom up excluding something special such as emergent, very technical, or very painful tasks to accomplish. (Conditional = On the condition that it does not hurt the public interests.)

For example, in consumer research, we ask difficult/technical questions to experts instead of consumers. Consumers are not the right persons to ask for technical/difficult questions because they will not have or will not come up to right answers based on our logics. We can use the same wisdom of Marketing Research in this context. We use Qualitative research method when questions get technical or difficult. The same thing should be true for democracy. We should ask opinion of group of experts when we are facing difficult or painful problems to solve. We can use jury system here, for example. We may pick up about 8 persons of experts in related fields and ask them to come up with a recommendation. Until they come up with a unanimous decision, discussion will not end, for example. In other words, please do not ask difficult questions to lay persons such as the general public when we are making difficult or painful decisions such as right now. This is an example of conditional democracy I am recommending. Under conditional democracy, we do not blindly ask opinions to the public. Instead we use a unanimous recommendation of experts when and only when questions or problems are difficult/painful. Nobody likes to take pains and thus democracy will be dysfunctional when we try to take pains or make painful decisions. In other words, we will eliminate an option of not paying back, delaying payments, or going for default from our choice set in the beginning.

<Democracy relies on logical thinking and logical behavior.>
<Democracy only works properly when healthy and normal conditions.>
(When healthy, democracy.)
(When unhealthy, non-democracy = some interventions, adjustments.)

<Mechanism of Human Body Function>

When human beings are under peace and healthy condition, human brain is in charge, which means that we think and act logically. However, when emergency or our survival is threatened, animal brain takes over control, which means we think and act illogically.

<Diagnosis first and application next.>
Is our current situation normal or not?
Difficult question is when to switch or how we judge whether the situation is normal or emergency. What about in between, which is semi-normal? Most likely our current situation is semi-normal, isn't it? What are we supposed to do? In other words, democracy only works well when peace and healthy conditions. When people are panic or emergency situation, democracy will not work well because people often times think and behave illogically.
Here, I am proposing conditional democracy to use when semi-emergency situation right now.

Background:

1. Changing Environment / Population Growth:
   World population has grown tremendously and now we have about 7.3 billion people on earth in 2015. World population in 1950 was about 2.5 billion (Angus Maddison). Our population was tripled in the past 65 years. Population of 7.3 billion is of course the highest in the human history.
   In 1 AD, the world population estimate is only 170 million. (Angus Maddison) This is roughly 43-times increase of the world population in the past about 2015 years.

   <The World Population is exploding.>

   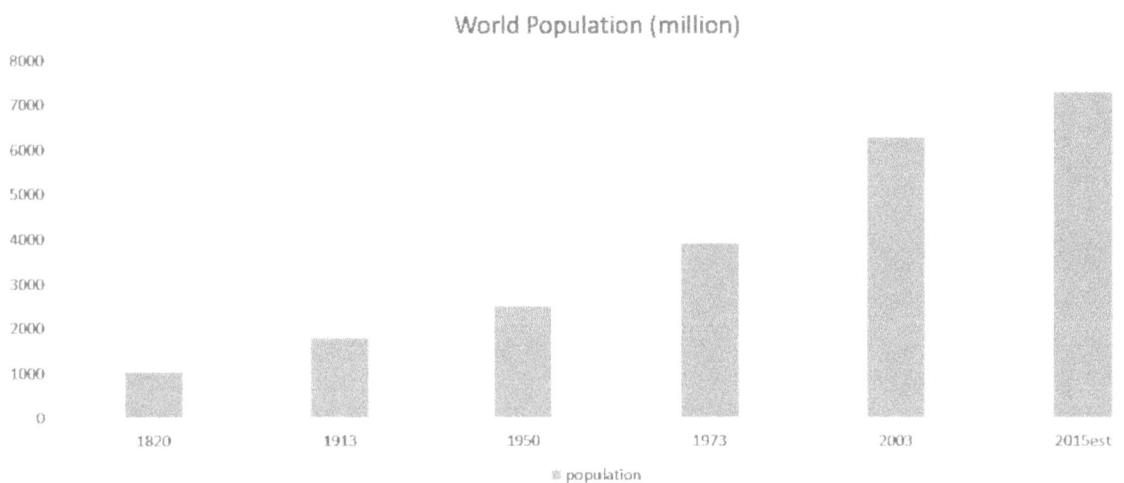

   (Graph 1, World Population. Data Source: combinations of the followings: Angus Maddison and Internet)

   We have too many fishes in a pond situation right now. What will happen when a pond is too crowded with too many fishes? Eventually lots of fishes will start dying and in the worst case, all fishes will die in the end. Why? Because when natural balance gets lost, self-regulating mechanism would not work and a vicious cycle will start. Things get worse and worse until whole things are over.

   Note: Do you see that we obviously have limitations on population growth?

On the contrary, our assumptions or fundamental premises of free economy is no limitations. Population growth positively affect economic prosperity up to some point or within a certain range.

When we use up some of natural resources such as fossil energy, it will paralyze a whole economy which is going to happen in the near future. Anyway, our assumptions of no limitations are obsolete, unfit, and totally inadequate from now on considering our current situations. We have to change it. We can no longer apply our current economics theory on the real world as it is. We have to run simulations before using it one by one, which is a test of its usability. We are applying economics theory inappropriately right now.

2. The Climate Change:

   I will not go into details on this topic since it takes too long. I just would like to point out one thing only. Human beings are parasites to the Earth since no other animals omit pollutions such as CO_2. The Climate Change is mainly created by CO_2 and thus by human beings. In other words, there must exist a very strong correlation between number of population and amounts of CO_2 emissions. If we invert this logic, we get the followings:

   <A Real cause is the population growth.>
   <A Symptom is the Climate Change.>

   If we can stop the population growth, we can stop this vicious cycle. If we don't stop the population growth, the vicious cycle will never end.

   By the way, according to Adam Smith, populations will grow to the extent of subsistence. This means that as long as we can provide basic necessities, namely foods, populations will keep growing.

   Lots of experts predict that the world population will grow around 10 billion in the coming 30 years or so. This is scary but this is the reality we have to face.

   In history, we never have been successful for controlling population by ourselves. However, we have to do it. Otherwise, calamities such as wars, famines, diseases, or the climate change will take care of it which was the case in the past.

3. Resources are running out:

Ms. Ellen MacArthur mentioned that coals will be running out in 118 years or so. According to Dr. Laurence Smith's book (British Geological survey 2005, about 10 years ago), oil will be in 42(42-10=32), Natural gas will be in 60(60-10=50), etc. Oil will be running out in 32 years and Natural gas will be running out in 50 years. However, please do not get panicked. I also got information from Mr. Gore's project such that solar and wind energy are very promising. I checked further to Lester Brown's book, "The Great Transition", I am positive that we can shift from Fossil Fuels to Solar and Wind Energy in time.

Note: In economy, this is a limitation. This is a violation of fundamental premises of economics theory such as abundant resources, which means that free economy model is not fitted for our current and future conditions.

When resources are limited, this condition works as a limitation, obviously.

According to the use instructions which are basic assumptions in case of economics theory, we are not supposed to apply free economics model when there exist limitations. This is what basic assumptions say. In the real world, limitations are not considered when applying the current economics theory. In other words, it is wrong to apply the current economics theory of purely mathematical when there exist limitations such as our situations right now.

(CIRCULAR ECONOMY)

What is fitted? CIRCULAR ECONOMY seems to be well fitted, although I only heard the concept of it.

Actually when there exist very sever constraints or limitations, such as inside of human body, where some gains must come from at the expense of some loss or compensation of the other parts in the body, there are no such things as free consumption, nor all you can consume, etc. Nothing is free of charges. Everything costs something. Or we can only gain something at the expense of something else. In this situation, only balance or equilibrium counts or matters. What are we willing to sacrifice in order to gain economic well-beings or prosperity and to what extent? Right now we are maximizing economic prosperity based on consumption-driven free economy. Since there exist limitations such as limited resources, we will be using up natural resources very quickly and we will suffer a great deal later in 100 years or so. This is the price we have to pay for using consumption driven economy when there exist limitations such as right now. Unless we control our economic prosperity somewhat in a way of using regulations of both incentives and dis-incentives, we will not be able to balance the two or reach to an equilibrium where we want to achieve. In other words, we have to give up current economics models for maximizing economic prosperity, although this is next to impossible as far as I know. This is similar to arms race, economic prosperity race, or reproduction race, which is our animal nature or embedded in our body as genes. However, anything is possible and nothing is impossible as long as we have a will and willing to sacrifice something instead. In the past, wars took care of it. Wars worked like re-booting mechanism of PC in the past by cleaning up or destroying something and ended up creating room for expansion such as after war demands. Scrap and build in a sense. This is more painful way of doing it, although this might be inevitable.

Introduction

From Nations to the Globe.

1. Fundamentally changed world:

    <From Nations to Global.>
    <From independent nation to global (interconnected with each other).>
    Our world has been changed fundamentally since Adam Smith's era when the Wealth of Nations Books were published around 1776, which is the same year as that of America's Declaration of independence. This is not a coincidence as far as I read between sentences in Adam Smith's books. Most likely he wanted to make sure that his theory/logic still holds after America's independence in 1776. Most of his books were written before it. By the way, basic unit of economy was a nation at that time.
    We can tell it from the title of his book such as "nations."
    Incidentally, assumptions of current economics theory are also single nation as opposed to global market such as now. In other words, since the current economics model is a single nation economics model, it should only be applied on a confined single country market.
    On the other hand, right now by looking at internet world, our economy is highly connected such as WWW (World Wide Web).
    Our economy is clearly global. Nations are highly inter-connected and thus we can no longer assume or treat "a nation" as a basic economic unit, which is obvious.
    Therefore, application of the economics theory on global market is violation of its use instructions. Only one way for me to make sense is that applying economics theory on the earth basis, which is a perfectly confined market and thus perfectly satisfy the assumption on this matter.
    Note: The fundamental assumption of economics theory is a confined market such as a pond situation, water in a glass situation, or a unit of single country. A Unit of "a Nation" is no longer satisfactorily confined as a market to apply economics theory right now. For example, when the U.S. expanded money supply after 2007-2008 financial crises, monetary reserve of the other

countries also increased accordingly. This means there exists a leakage or the U.S. economy is not confined in a single nation right now, which is very obvious.

When the U.S. expanded money supply, money reserves of whole world also expanded as follows:

<Money Reserves of Whole World.>

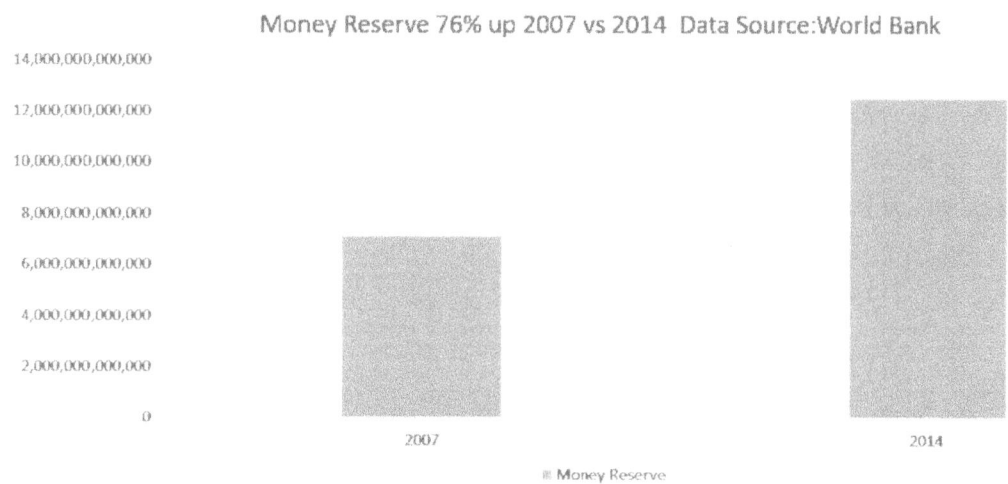

(Graph 2, Money Reserves. Data Source: World Bank.)

<Whole World>
7,112 billion $ in 2007   V.S.   12,518 billion $ in 2014. (76% up)
The above shows money reserves of the whole world.
Total Reserves (includes gold, current US$)

<China>
1,546 billion $ in 2007   V.S.   3,900 billion $ in 2014. (152% up)

<Japan>
976 billion $ in 2007   V.S.   1,260 billion $ in 2014. (29% up)
 (Data source: worldbank.org)

Applying a single country economics model on current global nations is unfit and inappropriate. If we want to do it, we need to apply it on the earth basis.

2. Economics theory is a mathematical model or logics:
   <Economics theory only works properly under healthy conditions.>

   Economic theory is basically mathematics, which is 100% true in case of micro economics. You will see only mathematical formulas or equations when you take micro economics classes at graduate level. In case of Macro- economics, logics is being used, which means that we have to choose either true (1) or false (0) based on logical thinking. You can see some pitfalls here. What if people act illogically? Economics theory will not work properly because basic assumptions include logical thinking and logical behavior. I will come back to this point later again since this is very important point when dealing with economics theory. People think and act illogically when emergency or at panic situation. Anyway, when handling mathematics or economics theory we need to secure pure and closed environment such as water in a cylinder, water in a cup, or water in a pond situation. In reality or in the real world it is impossible to secure a pond environment by 100%. In Adam Smith's era, a unit of a nation must be close enough for a pond environment. However, it is no longer the case now because a nation has many economic connections which are acting as holes or leakages. As a result, a unit of a nation is no longer suitable or satisfactory for being used as an economic unit.

   Basic Assumptions of Free Economy:
   <Use Instructions.>

   Most likely you have heard of basic assumptions of economics theory already. When I first heard about it, I thought something is very wrong with it because there is no way for us to meet such kind of pure conditions in the real world:

   <No limitations.>
   - Perfect information flow
   - Abundant resources. (It is not true anymore and thus Growth model is unfitted.)
   - Free movement of money, resources, and people, etc.

- Free fluctuations of exchange rate. This is also included now since current economy is global.

<When Using Mathematics>

- Logical thinking and behaviors.

    This is only true when conditions are normal or healthy. (When it is not normal and unhealthy, free economy is not fitted such as when emergency and war situation,)

<Realities>

   A. Limited Resources (Violation):
   Resources are no longer abundant anymore.
   As most people are aware of it, natural resources are running out very shortly. According to Dr. Laurence C. Smith's book, "The world in 2050," Oil will be running out in 42 years, copper in 35 years, zinc in 24 years (geological survey 2005), etc. You see that we have issues on natural resources which are limitations. We obviously need to revise or update the assumptions. I have seen limitation computer models in productions and management class at UCR. We can use that concept here. We need to apply limitations on economics models. In other world, we have to apply simulation programs on every economics model to see if the same conclusion is true when having limitations. Actually we can also apply our logics and can come up with some idea when applying limitations one by one as long as it is not very complicated.

   B. Imperfect information flow (Violation):
   There is no such thing as perfect information flow in the real world. Information could be beautifully hidden. Due mainly to computerization and information overflow based on human being's point of view, it is very easy to hide critical information or make it incomprehensible for laypersons which is proved in the sub-prime loan

incidence in 2008. Still, for the purpose of securing fair plays or fair competitions, somebody needs to watch for its fairness. In this respect, we need to have a Global "Fair Trade Committee "on internet or cyber space/world to begin with. The Current "Fair Trade Committee of independent nations" are not good enough to prevent unfairness or enforce farness due mainly to jurisdictional limitations. We need to have a "Fair Trade Committee of the Earth Government" in order for securing free information flow and/or preventing unfair practices. In other words, we have to prevent cheating.

C. Free flow of money? Not really:
When economic unit was a nation, currency such as US$ was good enough to secure free flow of money in one economic unit. Unfortunately, now it is no longer the case if we take a look at "Bit Coins" on internet. We need to have this kind of cyber money on global or the Earth basis, especially on internet environment. We need to have the Earth (cyber) money issued by the Earth government, which is non-existent yet.

D. Obstructions for Free Fluctuations of Exchange Rate (Violation):
As far as I checked, China is controlling Yuan's exchange rate in a certain range. Since China is not using free economy from the beginning, it is natural or common practices for her to manipulate exchange rate but it is a violation of the assumptions for free economy. This is one of the reasons why self-adjusting mechanism is not working properly right now with respect to the trade imbalance between the U.S. and China.

E. Normal and healthy conditions (Violation) :

Free economy or economics model/theory only works properly under normal conditions or healthy states. Since the assumptions are logical thinking and behaviors in case of mathematics or logics, which economics theory relies on, the conditions matter. For example, people think and act logically under healthy and normal conditions.

Therefore, economics theory or mathematics can be applied as it is. On the contrary, when panic or unhealthy conditions, people think and act illogically. In this case, we have to do something about it when conditions are unhealthy and not normal. Monopoly situation is unhealthy state in case of free economy and thus it must be rectified properly. For example, what would you do when you get sick? You go to see a doctor, right? Then you take a medicine or take a surgery. In case of economy, regulations works like a medicine. Wars or after war settlements work like medical operations. This is also true for democracy. Democracy never function well or properly under war situations. In war or abnormal situations, top-down command system such as military system needs to be applied instead. So is the case with economic system. When economy is sick or unhealthy such as monopolistic conditions exist in the markets, most likely regulations need to be applied first. If it did not work well, operations such as breaking-down of monopoly into a couple of pieces should be considered. Governmentalizing monopolistic companies by the Earth Government should also be considered as an option.

Body

Chapter 1: Starting from Adam Smith.

1. Starting from Adam Smith in 1776.
   Nothing is wrong with Adam Smith's theory or logics. Since our environment has been changed since Adam Smith's era, we need to adjust it accordingly.
   Since keeping a proximity to basic assumptions have got next to impossible now, we need to re-consider how to adjust it for the fundamentally changed world such as global economy or the Earth economy now.

   <Economics theory only works properly in a confined market. >
   In Adam Smith's era, Nations are fairly a good economic unit or a confined market. In this case, it is nothing wrong to apply a single country economics theory on nations even though basic assumptions are not met by 100%. Yes, I am aware of the existence of colonies such as America and West Indies. I tend to believe that Adam Smith also wanted to make sure that his theory/logics still works after America's declaration of Independence. Actually most of his books were written before the declaration of independence such as mentioned "Oct. 1773 (present)." In the end, his book was published in 1776, which was the same year as that of the declaration of independence.
   We know that economics theory never works for 100% when it is applied on the real world. What I am saying is that a Nation as an economic unit at Adam Smith's era was a more confined and closer to a cylinder environment than the current environments of nations which are being economically interwoven globally.

   <Application>
   <We need to apply economics theory on the earth basis now.>
   In other words, if we want to apply a single country economics theory in the real world now, we need to apply it on the Earth basis.

This is next to impossible since we do not have an Earth Government yet. The second best thing we can do is that we can apply it in a special district where basic assumptions of free economy can be held as much as possible. Most practical way of doing it may be as follows:
- Create a Cyber Earth Government in the United Nations.

- The Earth Government should issue Cyber Earth Government money, which is almost identical to that of Bit Coins on internet.

- The earth government should collect fair amount of taxes from where reasonable amounts of taxes are uncollectable right now such as at TAX Heavens countries. There should be no tax heavens for the Cyber Earth Government.
- There exists no issue of jurisdictions. The Cyber Earth Government can handle surveillance of fair trades such as Fund Money and "Earth Inc. (Mr. Al Gore, "The Future")" Actually, I borrowed terminology of "the Earth" from Mr. Gore's book.

2. Concept of "conditional".
   I tend to believe that we are familiar with conditional probability in mathematics. It is a given situation. I am very sure that we can use this concept of "conditional" on economics theory, too.
   "Conditional" means limitations and regulations in this context.

<Concept of free economy>

   Free Economy under healthy and normal conditions.

   "Everyman, as long as he does not violate the laws of justice, is left perfectly free to pursue his own interest his own way…." ("The Wealth of Nations".)

<Concept of conditional free economy>
   It is free on the condition that it does not hurts the public interests.

   Conditional free economy under unhealthy or abnormal conditions.

   Basic assumptions of conditional free economy:

- On the condition (given) that resources are limited.

Ms. Ellen MacArthur came up with a concept of CIRCULAR ECONOMY on this scarce resources' conditions, for example.

- On the condition that economic states are not normal or unhealthy/sick.

When economic conditions are not normal, effective regulations and laws need to be applied instead of letting it completely free by using free economy, which is laissez-faire.

<Circular Economy under severely restricted conditions.>

For example, there exists trade imbalance between the U.S. and China for the past thirty years or so. It is obvious that self-adjusting mechanism of free economy is not working properly right now.

In other words, market conditions are not healthy and thus it is not wise to let it be.

This is the same as human health conditions. When we are healthy, we do not need any medications. Free Economy is fine or better under normal and healthy conditions.

Conversely, when we get sick, we are better off taking some medications. In this context, medications are equivalent to regulations or laws. These regulations and laws have to be applicable on the Earth basis and thus these have to be governed by the Earth Government, or Cyber Earth Government.

<Monopolies = Unhealthy>

<Monopoly vs Fair Trade or Healthy Environment>

<Monopolies make market unhealthy.>

Note: I use monopolies in this book meaning that monopoly, duopoly, and oligopoly.

Everybody knows that monopolies are bad because the market become stagnant, which has been already proven in micro-economics theory. I have seen a monopoly model in micro-economics class taught by Dr. Mark Johnson at UCR. I would like to explain it in a practical point of view as follows:

    A. Monopoly can control production or supply.
    B. Monopoly can control or manipulate price.
    C. Monopoly can enforce anything it wants.

    A. Control supply.
    If only one company supply goods to whole world, what will happen if it stops providing goods? It can control supply. Consumers will suffer without any goods.

    B. Control price.
    Price goes up when short of supply situation occurs on the condition that demand stays the same. Everybody knows that when goods are in shortage, price goes up. A Monopoly can create this condition very easily as it wishes. A monopoly can control price.

    C. Tyranny.
    A monopoly can enforce its ego to customers. In other words, a monopoly can become the King and enforce consumers to become beggars.
    I do not want to see this kind of situations and so do you. Have you noticed that this kind of thing is already happening on our business environments right now?

    Adam Smith also says in his book that, "It is thus that the single advantage the monopoly procures to a single order of men is in many different ways hurtful to the general interest of the country."

In other words, we have to avoid monopolies which we are not successful right now because we can no longer control earth companies and fund money without having an earth government. Only the earth government can enforce anti-monopoly laws on global market basis to control or prevent monopolies.

<Conditional Economy under limitations.>

- It is free on the condition that individual interest does not hurt the public interests.

<Free economy under no limitations.>

In free economy theory, everybody just needs to mind his/her own business because everything else will be taken care of itself. I do not believe it. This is a bottom up approach. When there are no limitations, it could work because we can stretch out to infinity in order to create or make up the whole shape.
Right now we are facing to lots of limitations as follow:

- The Earth itself is geographically limited, of course. There aren't much room for expansion anymore.
- Natural resources are limited. We will use up oil in 30 years or so.

<Scarce resources are given condition.>

As you can see that these are given conditions such as conditional probability in mathematics. Conditional probability is different from normal probability since one action or a fact is already given. By the same token, we can no longer afford to let everybody acts completely free. There must be conditions for that or limitations.

American Economic System has worked very well since 1950's or after the WWII.

Yes, Free Economy System worked great but it was also supported by moral/ethics of Christianity in my opinion. Christian moral/ethics worked as a self-controlling mechanism in the past in the U.S. (I got this sense from Mr. Munger's book.) Do you realize that if everybody has very strict self-regulating rules, morals .and ethics, we do not need any laws and regulations?

I am talking about people of war generation those who experienced and survived the WWII such as Mr. Munger.

Unfortunately it is not the case anymore since the condition has been changed.

<Free economy is not appropriate under unhealthy conditions.>

Free economy or laissez faire only works well under healthy conditions and no limitations.

Our economic conditions are no longer healthy and thus ethics are no longer good enough to prevent monopolistic and forceful conducts in terms of fairness in business, for example. By the way, anti-monopoly laws and regulations are not working properly due mainly to jurisdictional constraints under global economy these days. This is one of the reasons why our market is unhealthy right now and free economy is unfit. Only the Earth government can enforce anti-monopoly laws to monopolies in global market in my opinion.

<Fund Money is making financial markets unhealthy.>

Concept of Fund Money:

Concept of Fund Money itself is to take advantage of economy of scale or monopolistic power. In my opinion, this concept itself is questionable from the beginning. Right now, nobody or no single government can control activities of Fund Money (on cyber world) due mainly to jurisdictional issues and short of high-tech competency. As far as I know, we do not have any global or The Earth regulations controlling fund money activities. Fund Money is acting like sharks in the ocean. Individual investors are like swimmers on the beach. Individual swimmers (investors) get bitten by sharks very often these days. For, example, I got bitten very badly by a company together with Fund Money by forcefully overtook my stocks which I kept for future growth potential. I could have suited it because some people suited it. Instead, I decided to stay away from financial markets forever. Financial markets are no longer healthy in my opinion and experiences. Fair competitions are no longer protected in my opinion.

Can you see that? This is not a fair play or fair trade anymore. This is not a fair competition. Analogy is a boxing match between a heavy weight boxer and a light weight boxer, for example. A light weight campion boxer can never win against a heavy weight boxer no matter how good he or she is. We need to have global or the Earth regulations for controlling Fund Money, which has a sort of monopoly position, for enforcing a fair play.

When we deal with a computer, we oftentimes lose human touch. This could be the reasons why human ethics or Christian ethics do not work well on cyber world when looking at the forceful acts of Fund Money in financial markets where transactions are basically one click away.

<Growth Model of financial markets.>

<Monetary System>

<Collateral of gold and silver.>

A. Adam Smith's Era (Money was linked with precious metals such as gold and silver by 100%):

In Adam Smith's era, mainly coins such as silver coins and gold coins were being used in commerce. Coinage can prevent counterfeit and improve smooth, easy, and reliable exchanges/transactions but coinage also incur some costs. In case of coins, there exists issue of torn-out and thus re-coinage is necessary, which is a huge burden to any government. Mainly for this reason, paper money has got available as a Bank's promissory note which is directly linked to such as silver bullion or gold bullion in the coffer of the bank. In other words, money or currency is 100% linked to physical

collateral such as silver and gold at Adam Smith's era in Europe. (Exception is the U.S. In the U.S. or American colonies of Europe at Adam Smith's era, paper money was already being used. I also admits that I have no idea how it worked in American colonies at that time.) In this way, government or bank can circulate money to the extent it has silver, gold, or some precious metals in the coffer. Yes, there exist limitations in this monetary system.
This is one of the reasons why America was discovered if I am not mistaken. European people at that time looked for wealth outside of Europe such as good lands for agriculture, animals (beasts), and precious metals.
Precious metals such as golds and silvers are the third objective when looking for new lands/worlds according to Adam Smith's opinion. People in Europe needed more and more of golds and silvers for commerce and thus accumulation of golds and silvers meant accumulation of wealth. European people were looking and searching for silvers and golds and yes they found silver and gold mines in America.(Adam Smith, "Wealth of Nations",) "America" in this context means whole American continent including not only USA but also central and south America. Actually values of silver in England/Europe dramatically decreased due to discovery of silver (and gold) mines in America in Adam Smith's era.

<Money is 100% linked with gold and silver in Adam Smith's era.>

My point here is that all currency/money are linked with precious metals by 100% in Adam Smith's era.

<Money has almost no link or no collateral now.>

(Nixon Shock in 1971.)

B. Current Monetary System (Almost no link with precious metals):
(Money is just perceived value without almost any link with precious metals right now.)

As you know, there is no direct link between paper money ($) and gold or precious metals right now. I remember "Nixon shock" declaring abandonment of link between the U.S. $ and gold in 1971. Currencies were freely floating by 1973.

Since commerce has grown so big and there might be no way of linking dollars to gold reserves, Nixon Shock occurred based on my educated guess.

However, I also suspicious about that the U.S. must start having trouble for clearing national debts around this time. The U.S. has been making trade deficits since 1953 according to the data I collected.

It goes to Breton woods and IMF (International Monetary Fund), basket of currencies for security, etc. What does this mean? Money or the U.S. $ has become just perceived value based on trust/credit worthiness without actual possession of collaterals such as gold for exchange.

My point here is that there is almost no link between the U.S. $ and gold and thus there is no limit of printing the U.S. $ unless something happens.

Adam Smith says in his book that balance of trade is very important. I do not recall that the U.S. had trade surplus for a long time.

In spite that the U.S. has had trade deficits for a long time, how could the U.S. manage to pay for the Trade Deficits for such a long time? Printing the U.S. $?

No. As far as I checked it, the U.S has been doing it by borrowing money, which is recommended by economists, right? Which is issuing the U.S. treasury bonds if I am not mistaken. When I checked my notebook of Dr. Auerbach's class in 1986, Dr. Auerbach also recommended borrowing money for financing because it does not increase interest rate. He is right and economists are right of course that borrowing money does not increase interest rate. However, the evidence shows that it increased interest payment in amounts since compound interest rate worked very harshly. This is the rule of capitalism, right? With compound interest rate, total debt amounts get doubled in 20 years or so, which happened in case of the U.S. national debts. It is no wonder that the U.S. has about "$18 trillion of aggregate debts." (Victor Davis Hanson, "Remembering Who We Are")

<Some Math.>

Let's see we have about 7.3 billion people on earth.
The U.S. has about 0.3 billion population.
18,000,000,000,000 / 300,000,000 = $60,000 per person.
Interest payment alone is about 0.43 trillion $ a year, which means about $1400 a year per person. It is about 2.3% of interest rate. This is equivalent to $3.8 a day per person. We can eat a hamburger every day for lunch with this money or interest payment.
Yes, we have huge debts in Japan also.
Japanese government is imitating the U.S. and thus Japan is just a shadow. When the U.S. changes, Japan will change also and thus we have to change the U.S. first, which is my logics.

Do you know why this kind of things happen?
<A symptom: National Debts.>
<A real cause: Over spending>
<Debts: Spending > GDP/Income (what we produce)>

    A. There is no link between the U.S. $ and gold.
    B. Consumption driven economy

A. There is almost no link between the U.S. $ and gold.
   <No anchor for expansion >
   <Overspending>

     In Adam Smith's era, in case of trade deficits, silver and gold bullions go out to abroad. What will happen if a country does not have enough golds and silvers to pay for the debts to the other countries? No more transactions will be taken place or the country will become insolvent immediately, right?

<Origin of commerce>

     We started commerce by barter, right?
     This is a starting point.
     In case of barter, when we have nothing to exchange, there is no deal or no commerce.
     In other words, what we produce = what we consume.

We cannot spend more than what we produce in nature.

In Adam Smith's era, if we do not have enough golds and silvers, we cannot buy things.

No gold/money, no deal or no trade.

What about now?

Link between gold and paper money got cut.

What will happen?

Clever, isn't it?

Paper money works like that of credit card or postponement of payment.

I owe you.

For example, the U.S. government owe you/us in case of issuing the U.S. treasury bonds and selling them to you/us.

We are using double ledger of accounting, right?

When the U.S. government owes you, the national debt goes up.

This is a way of financing by borrowing.

This is the reason why the U.S. government accumulated national debts of about 18 trillion dollars so far if I am not mistaken.

It is possible when the President Nixon declared abandonment of link or reserve of gold for the U.S. $, there must had been no other way of doing it. Since the U.S. $ is global currency, there are lots of room to be reserved or kept as money reserves in many countries, most likely more than 150 countries.

(Trade Balance)

By the way, Adam Smith emphasizes the importance of trade balance many times in his book.

Trade balance of a country is equivalent to balance between income and spending in a family. Basically we can't spend more than what we make/produce.

One of the way is borrowing money, which is the same case with the U.S. Government. Only problem of borrowing money is compound rate of interest. This is a danger of capitalism, right? If you leave borrowed money unpaid for 20 to 30 years, the amount will get doubled based on compound rate of 3% interest. Even the U.S. government can't beat Capitalism.

Compound rate of interest will kill the U.S. government in 30 years or so if we do not handle it very quickly and properly.

"It is true that everybody just needs to mind his or her own business." However, if I read Adam Smith's sentences between the lines, each government or legislator of a government still needs to pay a severe attention to the balance of trade; otherwise, a country will go bankrupt or become insolvent in Adam Smith's era.

In my opinion, when conditions are unhealthy, it is wrong to assume that everything will be taken care of itself because an invisible hand will work. Invisible hand only works under healthy conditions such as no interventions, etc. Or, invisible hand will not work timely when intervention exists and thus it might work too late in a painful way in the end. We had two world wars and one great depression after implementation of Adam Smith's theory or free economy, laissez-faire. Self-adjusting mechanism includes wars, war economies, and depressions also as you may have noticed.

Let's take an example of human health analogy. When we suspect catching a cold, it is better to take some measures such as taking enough rest at early enough.

Go to bed early and take enough sleep for a couple of days as a precaution. If we do it early enough, we do not need any medications because healing mechanism will or may work. (Laissez-faire will be fine since self-adjusting mechanism will work.)

On the contrary, if we ignore this symptom and push ourselves too hard (while suppressing symptoms by taking alleviating medicines), we might be ended up developing pneumonia. In other words, we can rely on laissez-faire at certain degree/range only or under healthy conditions. Before situations get overwhelming, we have to do something about it.

We need to start cutting or reducing the national debts right now. In other words, we need to stop borrowing and start making our ends meet.

In my opinion, each government is responsible for watching for the trade balance.

How are we going to do it? Benjamin Franklin Campaign, in my opinion, which will be explained later on.

Chapter 2: Consumption driven economy.
1. Consumption driven economy will be a bad choice from now on.

   In my opinion, our current troubling situation is also something to do with the consumption driven economy. In other words, spending is recommended and good for facilitating our economy.
   This is true from economic point of view.
   From broader perspective or a bird's eye point of view, consumption driven economy is no longer justifiable due mainly to shortage of our resources. I am no longer talking about only economic point of view here.
   Now we have dual purposes in our life.
   One is economic prosperity and the other is our survivals as human beings.
   Since we are using up natural resources in the near future, consuming as much as possible by consumption driven economy is outdated, inappropriate, and self-killing.
   Logically speaking, it will cost us our lives in the long run.

2. Leeman Shock in 2008/ System Failure.
   Good example is the subprime issue of Leeman shock in 2008.
   > According to Manoj Singh, October 28, 2008, "to keep recession away, the Federal Reserve lowered Federal funds rate 11 times – from 6.5% in May 2000 to 1.75% in December 2001 – creating a flood of liquidity in the economy." "…by 2004, U.S. homeownership had peaked at 70%........during the last quarter of 2005, home prices started to fall….. many subprime borrowers now could not stand the higher interest rates and they started defaulting on their loans." "During February and March 2007, more than 25 subprime lenders filed for bankruptcy…" (http://www.investpedia.com/)

   This is because of combination of cheap money and bad loans based on my understanding from the above comments.

   Consumers are encouraged to buy luxurious cars and fancy houses based on overstretched installment plans. In this case, since critical information was technically hidden, it became possible to borrow huge money beyond his/her means, which is almost impossible to pay off under proper evaluations. In other words, this is cheating. It ended up that cheating was realized in due time and the Leeman went to bankrupt. Money was desperately in need to keep economy going or recession away. Otherwise, a great depression could have happened. As far as I know and read, the U.S. increased the money supply as much as three times since then in order to supply enough capital/money in the market, which worked well. Thank you very much. We have not suffered from another great depression so far. As a result, because of issuing lots of the U.S. Treasury bonds, the U.S. debts have been increased further. In other words, defaults or losses of the Leeman shock or this financial crisis were partially or mainly absorbed as an increase of the U.S. debts according to my educated guess.

But I may be wrong. Please double check it to financial analysts or economists on this matter. I am not a financial analyst nor an economist. I am just a generalist with broader but thin knowledges and experiences, instead.

These days majority of us are specialists and thus this is why not many people see things as a whole or from a bird-eye point of view.

Here I am explaining an overall broad point of view without going into details. Please check for details to specialists such as financial analysts or economists in this case. Actually, both generalists and specialists need to work together all the time.

3. Cruel Business System is creating the Last Man Standing Situation.

<Cruel business model of Publicly Traded Stock Companies.>

An American manager once told me that business is a war. A chairman of American company mentioned to us as follows:
"It is nice that we do not have to kill people (in business)."
I heard this phrase more than a couple of times during his and his management team's stay in Yokohama, Japan.

According to American business rule, company is for investors. (According to Mr. Munger.)

Because of growth business model, companies are expected to grow and increase both sales and profits every year such as 6% every year or even more as far as I know. While I was working for a subsidiary of an American Company in Japan, a boss of our president came to Japan from the U.S. headquarters and told us that we are two million dollars short (on budget) and we have to come up with something. As I was called up by a secretary of our president on the internal phone to come to the meeting room right away, there were only two persons there, our president and his American boss, who is most likely a regional president or a regional financial manager such as for Asia or Pan Pacific. I only knew him by his first name without his title. I heard the above story in that room when I was called up and joined that meeting. In less than about five minutes, our president Mr. HP asked his boss to talk about it in his office alone and I was discharged. In less than one hour or so, I was called up again by the secretary of Mr. HP to come to his office. There I was told that your (MY) expense budget was cut by one million dollars while keeping sales budget stay the same. You have to revise your budget and let's talk about how to do it right now. How are you going to do it? Which marketing plans do you want to keep? Do you know that except TV ADs and about 50% of magazine ADs, all the other expense budgets were cut on the spot in less than one hour and it became my new commitment according to Mr. HP, the president of the subsidiary company in Japan? It was done unofficially because the budget was already approved officially via proper annual procedures a couple months ago. Do you know that this is an inside deal between the two, which is a secret officially. This was a way for this American manager to save his job for a short period of time, may be a year or so. This is a kind of cheating in my opinion. In the end, these two persons killed the business which I was responsible for in a few years in my opinion.

By the way, I left this company after several months of this incidence because of my physical illness I have been suffering. Besides, I have seen enough dirty tricks already. After a year or so, I heard a story that Mr. HP had left the company because he could not get along well with his new boss. Well, do you think that this is democracy? No. But this is a reality in the business world as you know. Do you think that this works? Oh, yeah. At my position, I will not be fired but I am sure that I will be threatened to get fired. Actually Mr. HP told me several times that if he gets fired, he will fire me. This is a threat, right?

Most likely, I will be set aside from the main stream position if I do not meet my budget. This is not the case for upper management such as Mr. HP and his boss as you know. In case of upper management, managers will get fired very quickly. I knew a president of Japanese subsidiary got fired by a FAX from headquarters in N.Y. Actually, I saw him the very next morning since a meeting was scheduled. Before that meeting, I was told that Mr. R got fired yesterday by FAX. I could not say a word. I just thought that if I want to look for a position of his level, the same thing will happen to me someday.

I heard that a favorite phrase of Mr. Tramp is "You are fired."

In other words, budget must always work in business because it is not democracy at all.

Do you know why cheating occurs in business?

Because our jobs or means of our subsistence are being threatened. When basic needs are threatened, people get panic and think and act illogically because of our survival needs or instincts. In other words, our animal brains take control to save our basic needs such as foods, clothes, and shelters which we get from income/job when these are in danger.

This is an animal nature and thus also a nature of human beings.

What is wrong?

What is bad is not human beings/us.

What is bad is our cruel business system which is too demanding.

It demands growth forever exponentially while there exist clear limitations in front of us.

Putting into another words, the current business system is requesting us to achieve impossible things and thus we must change the system as follows:

4. Change the concept of the company.
    <Definition or Concept of the Company.>
    From: Companies are for investors. (Now)
    To: Companies are not only for investors but also for the public. (In the future)
    Where the public means human beings on the earth instead of just people of one country.

5. Unmanaged situations.

<Budget didn't work for government.>

When I took a macro-economics class by Dr. Auerbach, he told us as follows:
"We have trade deficits now. We tried budget but the budget didn't work." (At GSM, UCR in 1986.)
He shrugged his shoulder and smiled with a giving-up gesture.
He also said, "When country gets rich, people work less."
Bible says, "Work 6 days and take one day off." (Although I have never read the bible, sorry.)
How many days American people work these days?
Most likely between 4 and 5 days a week considering many holidays in addition to two days off in a week in the U.S..
Adam Smith says, labor can be divided into two classes.
Productive labor and unproductive labor.
(Note: Although I use the concept of productive and unproductive here, my categorization may be somewhat different from that of Adam Smith's.)
Working days are productive considering GDP or what we produce.
Weekends and holidays are unproductive since basically we do not work/produce and we do not contribute to GDP or what we produce on off-days and holidays.
When we do not have much money to spend, holidays are rather painful because we need to spend money on holidays. It is better off for us to work when we have no money to spend. This comes from my personal experiences in the US. I did not have much money to spend when I was studying in the U.S. I never looked forward to having holidays at that time because those were rather troublesome and painful for me.

With respect to the trade deficit issue, when Dr. Auerbach said that the budget didn't work, do you know what I did? I laughed.
Do you know why I laughed?
Most likely, it came from group mentality by thinking that I am not responsible for that as an individual.
Besides, I am not an American citizen and thus it is none of my business.
It is actually some of my business right now, though.

In case the U.S. declares defaults on the national debts, the world economy will most likely corrupt and then I will also greatly suffer.

Do you know why the budget did not work for the government?
Because it is democracy in my opinion.
Since politicians are elected by votes, nobody can fire them except the public. It can be done only in election.
Logically speaking, we cannot fire politicians under the democracy regardless of meeting the budget for the reduction of the national deficits or not, which is totally different from the company situation mentioned the above where the business system is not democracy.
We have a problem here.
If we use democracy system on the national debt issue, it will never get done quickly. Some America doctor predicted that it would take about 4700 years to pay it back based on a very reasonable scenario. However, it will never happen under democracy system since it did not happen for the past about 60 years or so since 1953 in my opinion.

6. The situation has never got better for at least the past 30 years or so.

<Continuous Trade Deficits since 1976 ("Trading economics") or even earlier. >

Things have not been changed since 1986 when I heard about the trade deficit issue from Dr. Auerbach.
It's been about thirty years since then.
The U.S. has been accumulating the trade deficits for the past thirty years or more since then.
According to Dr. Auerbach, there are three options for that looking at my notes in 1986 as follows:
1. Printing money
2. Borrowing.
3. Tax.

It is already proved that when printing money, it will cause inflation.
Germany experienced high-per-inflation in the past.

Dr. Auerbach recommended borrowing money because borrowing money will not increase interest rate.

Dr. Auerbach did not say much about taxing.

OK, borrowing money must be the best choice among the above three. Well, Dr. Auerbach is obviously very smart and also this is also an opinion of novel Laurate in economics and thus this must be it I thought at that time. However, this was only a temporal solution or postponement of payments based on the result and my findings later on.

1. Borrowing money did not increase interest rate but did increase interest payments in amounts due mainly to compound rate of interest.
2. Mechanism of capitalism or compound interest rate gives a serious impact in the long range such as 30 years of period. According to Mr. Munger, "…the elementary mathematics of compound interest-which is one of the most important models there is on ear."

    For example, $(1.03)^{30}=2.427$

    Suppose that interest rate is 3%. If we leave it for thirty years, it becomes 2.4 times of borrowed money in thirty years.

    Given that the U.S. has been creating trade deficits for the past thirty years or so continuously, the U.S. will end up paying for a lot more than the principal (the amounts actually borrowed), which is more than two times.

3. A Nation based economics theory (A single country economy model.)
    This means that self-adjusting mechanism works or theory works 100% when economics theory is applied in a confined market or in one nation.
    In other words, when the U.S. government borrows money from only the U.S. public and companies, borrowing money is just fine since lenders and borrowers are the same ultimately. (When everything is confined in the U.S.) Nothing changes as a whole. This is a zero-sum game. If somebody wins, somebody loses at the expense of the others at the same amounts. It only changes share/proportion of it.
    (Here I am excluding the growth factor. When the economy grows, everybody gains benefits because of its growth. This is why we use the growth model in economics.)
    Since the U.S. public and the U.S. companies own the U.S. government, when the U.S. government declares defaults, it does not change the

situation as a whole or as a nation. It only changes the proportion/share of burdens/debts within its economic unit, which is within the U.S. In other words, the debts will go or be passed on from the U.S. government to individual creditors in the U.S.

This is not the case now anymore. When I checked increase of money Supply M1 and M2 in the U.S., money reserves of the other nations also increased. I also know that many foreign governments buy the U.S. treasury bonds. The U.S. borrows money by selling the U.S. treasury bonds. This means that actually the U.S. is borrowing lots of money from foreign governments now. This is violation of assumptions of a nutshell environment since interest payment goes out from the U.S., which is a bleeding in human analogy.

(Necessity of Positive Trade Balance)

Trade deficit is also a bleeding in human analogy.
Trade balance is the same as family balance sheet.
It is a balance between export and import.
Export is the same as sales and import is purchasing.
If you import more than exports/sales, you get a trade deficit.
At Adam Smith's era, a trade deficit was paid by golds and silvers.
If you do not have enough golds and silvers, you can't buy or imports will be restricted.
This is not the case in the U.S. right now since we are using paper money ($) without linking gold.
This is both good and bad.
We can get lots of leverage but we also lose an anchor.
Now money is just perceived value based only on trust and credibility. Once we lose credibility, it will backfire.

Chapter 3: Case Study Financial Crisis in 2007-2008.
The U.S. had a financial crisis situation in 2007-2008.

Priori: This is just a tip of iceberg and the real causes are as follow:

1. The U.S. Trade deficits in the past thirty years or more. (A bleeding in human analogy)
2. Logarithmic increase of Compound Interest Rate.
3. Self-adjusting mechanism only works in free economy under healthy conditions. An invisible hand will not work with China, which uses government-controlling economy. The trade imbalance between the U.S. and China will not get better since China is most likely controlling exchange rate in a fixed range.
4. The current economics model based on growth is obsolete and inadequate.
5. Democracy only works in peace and healthy conditions. When emergency or semi-emergency situations, we need to come up with something different.
6. Alleviation of symptoms will not be good enough. We need to change everything fundamentally including system changes and life style changes in accordance with each other. The same system (process), the same result.

   1. <The U.S. debts>
   The U.S. debts have been increasing since at least 1953.
       1953: 275.2 (billion $)
       1986: 2,125.3 (billion $)
       2014: 17,824.1 (billion $)
   In the past about 60 years, it became about 65 times.
   In the past 28 years, it became about 8.4 times.

   <The U.S. Debts>

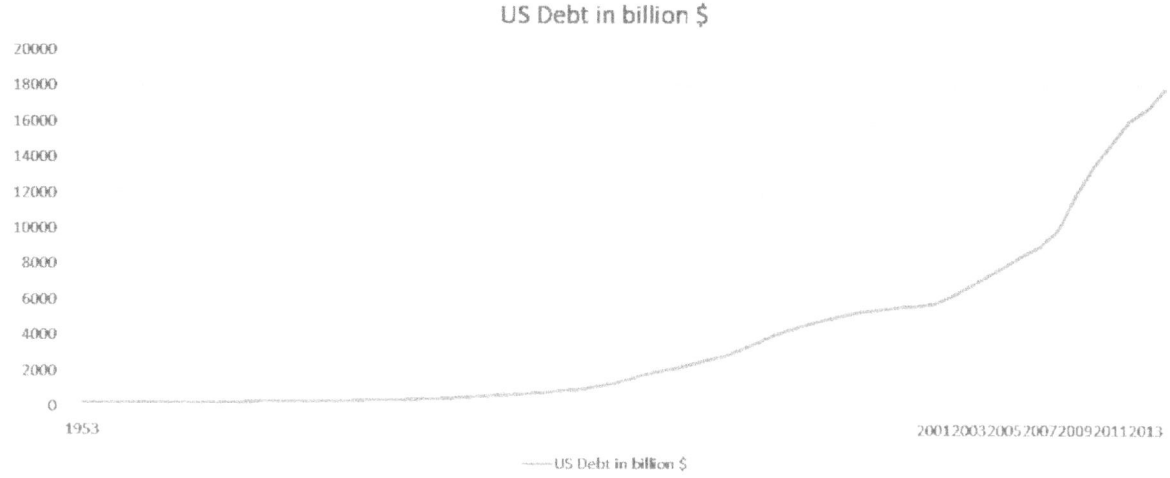

(Graph 3, the U.S. debts. Data Source: Treasurydirect.)

The above graph shows the U.S. debts from 1953 to 2014.
Increasing trend of the national debts has been skyrocketed since around 2007/2008 financial crisis, which is very scary.

(Note: The U.S. had national debts before 1953 such as since 1950 or earlier.)
(The U.S. National debts started skyrocketed from around Nixon Shock in 1971 when the U.S. abandoned link between the U.S. $ and gold based on my observation of looking at the above graph.)

Why?
There are always reasons behind it.
The followings are my explanations of the reasons:

2. Negative Trade Balance.
   The U.S. Trade Balance shows negative figures such as follows:

   2007 :   -701,423 (million $)

   2008:   -695,937
   2009:   -303,963
   2010:   -500,027
   2011:   -556,838
   2012:   -534,656
   2013:   -476,392

2014:   -504,711
(Data: US Census Bureau)

(Graph 4, the U.S. Trade Balance.)

Note: A negative trade balance once in a while is not so bad. However, it is bad to have a negative trade balance continuously such as the above. Trade balance is the same as corporate balance sheet (P/L) or family net balance between income and spending as follow:

Trade Balance = Exports (selling) – Imports (buying)

In case of the U.S., Imports (buying) always exceeds Exports (selling) for the past at least eight years.

Do you know that the U.S.'s Trade imbalance with China represents 68% of total in 2014?
In other words, if the U.S. solves an issue of trade imbalance with China, the U.S. will solve a majority of it.

3. The U.S. Trade Balance with China.

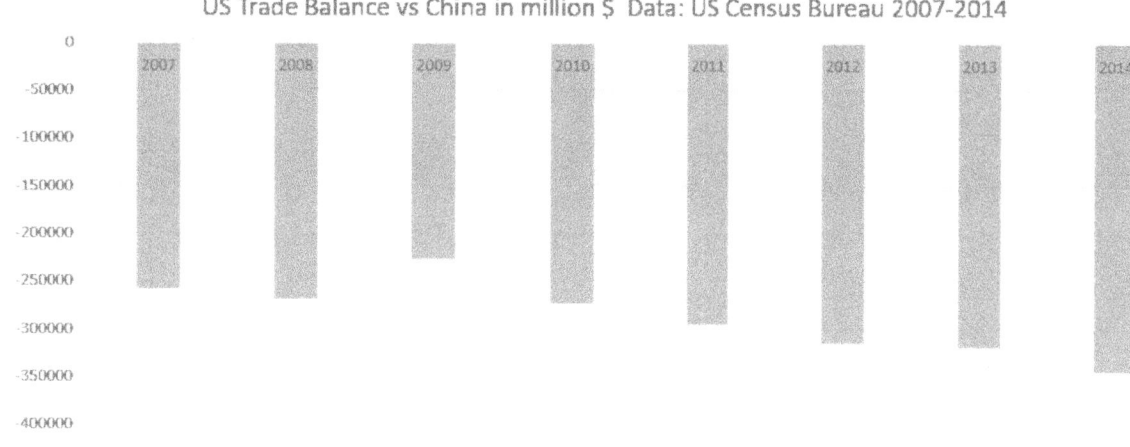

(Graph 5, the U.S. Trade Balance with China. Data source: US Census Bureau.)

The above graph shows the U.S. trade imbalance with China.

<Contribution of China to Total Trade Imbalance of the U.S.>

(Graph 6, China's contribution on the U.S. Trade Imbalance.)

Note: The above graph shows % of contribution China has on the negative trade balance of the U.S.'s.

As you can see from the above graph, China contributes to the majority of the U.S. negative trade balance such as 68% of it in 2014.

Conversely, unless the U.S. solves an issue of trade deficits with China, the trade deficit issue will never be solved.

The U.S. Trade imbalance with China

	(Trade Imbalance)	(Exchange Rate 1US $ to yuan)
1985	-6 (million $)	2.94
1986	-1164	3.45
1987	-2796	3.72
1988	-3489	3.72
1989	-6234	3.77
1990	-10431	4.78
1991	-12691	5.32
1992	-18309	5.51
1993	-22777	5.76
1994	-29505	8.35
1995	-33789	8.35
1996	-39520	8.31
1997	-49695	8.29
1998	-26927	8.28
1999	-68677	8.28
2000	-83833	8.28
2001	-83096	8.28
2002	-103065	8.28
2003	-124068	8.28
2004	-162254	8.28
2005	-202278	8.19
2006	-234101	7.98
2007	-258506	7.61
2008	-268040	6.95
2009	-226877	6.83
2010	-273042	6.78
2011	-295250	6.45
2012	-315103	6.31
2013	-318713	6.15

2014   -343079   N/A

<The U.S. Trade Balance with China.>

(Graph 6, the U.S. Trade Balance with China between 1985 and 2014.)

The U.S. trade deficits with China have been increasing basically for the past about 30 years.

Can you see that the U.S.'s situation has been getting really bad since around 1999? I tend to believe that this is something to do with dot com babble in the U.S. when lots of dot com companies went to bankrupt. In 1998, the U.S. economy showed a strong sign of recovery based on the above data but it was very short lived.

(Self-adjusting mechanism is not working.)
Can you see that strange movements between the two?
In free economy, self-adjusting mechanism should work.
When trade balance between the two expands like the above, exchange rate may or can adjust to offset it based on the theory of free economy or mechanism of an invisible hand.
It is not working at all here in the above.
By just looking at the above, the U.S. had a very minor trade deficit with China when exchange rate was at 1$ = 3 Chinese yuan in 1985. May be the U.S. can clear up trade imbalance with China at this kind of rate such as 1$ = 3 Chinese yuan.

Currently exchange rate is at 1$ = more than 6 Chinese yuan.
In other words, the U.S. dollar must be way too strong against Chinese yuan by taking a look at historical results of trade balance between the two countries such as the above.
If the U.S. devalues the U.S. $ by half against Chinese yuan, its side effect will be huge such as loss of the U.S. $ buying power as much as 50% or more against Chinese products.
Adam Smith includes manufacturing as productive labor and thus using China as manufacturing-hub for the U.S. must be logically unwise because China is gaining jobs(productive labor) at the expense of those of the U.S.'.

(Basics)
If we go back to basics, everything productive basically come from the Nature such as agriculture, fishery, forestry, mining, etc.
When we engage these industries, we can increase what we produce or GDP.
We call it the first level industry in Japan.
Did you notice that every subsistence comes from this first level industry? In other words, the size of a pie is decided by the amounts of produce from the Nature before the industrial revolution of 18th century. In Adam Smith's terminology, cultivation and improvement of land is most important for economic growth. After the industrial revolution, manufacturing is also very important considering subsistence as well as employment/jobs in any countries including the U.S. Since the U.S. gave this manufacturing jobs/employment to China, China increased subsistence which contributed to the population growth also in my understanding.
Why the U.S. companies shifted manufacturing to China? Because of the cruel business system. If I don't do it, somebody else will do it. Eat or be eaten. Grow or get fired. It is a war in business. In the end, we are making matters worse. We are taking away jobs from American workers and instead increased factory jobs in China. Chinese workers increased subsistence at the expense of that of American workers. These contributed to both population growth in China as well as south Asia at the expense of job/employment losses in the U.S.
What is bad? What is the real cause?

4. Real Causes of Dysfunctional Economy.

    1. Growth Model.
    2. Violation of the Use Instructions.

1. Growth model of business:
(Growth model of business is no longer fit for the current conditions.)
   Since investors are too demanding or allowed to be very demanding based on our current business system, companies have to increase both sales and profits at very high rate no matter what. As a result, the U.S. companies moved out production from the U.S. to mainly China looking for cheap labors in order to reduce COGS and thus increase competitive edges.

2. Violation of the Use Instructions:
   Logic of economics model:
   There are basically two factors to consider as follows:
   Production and consumption.
   What we produce (GDP) = Consumption.

   Adam Smith says that encourage production and consumption in order to facilitate economy. Economists use the factor of Interest for Production. When Interest goes down, Production goes up, for example. We use consumption driven economy to facilitate consumption. We facilitate both, which is logical.

   <A Swing of Pendulum.>
   My father used to say as follows:
   "When we have money, we do not have time. When we have time, we do not have money."
   This is true for most of time. Rich retired persons have both time and money, which is an exception. When I was studying in the U.S., I did not have neither time nor money, which was only short time of period, though. Anyway, there is a cycle of work and leisure. Work (Production) and Consumption (spending.) Make money and spend money.

We cannot keep spending forever.

<Basic Assumptions: A Confined market.>
Consumption driven economy:
Consume first and then we have to produce. Production goes up and Income goes up. Since we made money, we can spend money. Everything works perfectly in a confined market.

<Now what?>
Consume first in the U.S. Then we have to produce. In China Production goes up and Income goes up. In the U.S., Production may or may not go up and thus Income may or may not go up because there aren't many productions in the U.S. anymore. The U.S. borrows money and spend money again. There must be a healthy cycle of Production and Consumption in economy. This cycle is not working at all within a range of the U.S. market as opposed to the above mentioned healthy cycle. Here, the U.S. spends and China produces. The U.S. created huge national debts and China became very rich as a result. Why is that? Since this is the violation of the use instructions for the economics theory. The market must be confined since the theory is designed for a confined market. This is a system failure and thus we have to change it. One thing is true is that the U.S. needs to produce more and increase productive labor. Also the U.S. needs to spend less and reduce unproductive labor such as holidays.
By the way, this is not people's fault. People in the U.S. can no longer find factory jobs in the U.S. basically and thus nothing is wrong with people.

Fundamentally, it is the business system which demands forever growth without consideration of future consequences in advance. We need to change the business system which is no longer fit and self-killing. The current business system is getting more harmful than beneficial for us these days if I am not mistaken.

It will create the last man standing situation in the end, which is a monopoly. People and company will act based on fear. Eat or be eaten. This will lead us to animal behaviors trying to save our jobs and companies no matter what. This is basically the same as arms race. Everybody knows that we are better off without nuclear weapons. But because of fear, we cannot get rid of nuclear weapons.

By the same token, restricting M&A's is necessary in order to prevent or control monopolies in advance. M&A's are not natural growth. Adam Smith always recommends natural and gradual process. We will create monopolies more easily and quickly by allowing M&A's.

Therefore, conditional business model is recommended. In other words, we have to enforce anti-monopoly regulations by using an earth government.

5. Change the concept of the company.

<Change a definition or concept of companies.>

Companies are not only for investors but also for the public, who are human beings on the earth.
Since we clearly see future consequences of it, we should prevent monopolies by regulations such as anti-monopoly laws and regulations imposed by the earth government in the near future.

<Unproductive labor>

According to Adam Smith, menial servants are classified as unproductive labor because they do not increase the size of a pie or what we produce. In other words, we can live without it. We do not depend upon subsistence in this category and thus it is classified as unproductive labor by Adam Smith in my opinion. Although service sector is very important now, it has a very little contribution to our subsistence. Yes, it has a contribution of providing our jobs but it will not increase the size of a pie or surplus produce considering exports. In other words, domestic manufacturing can increase a chance of exporting and thus it is very important now in consideration of increasing exports which we want right now when decreasing the national debts. On the other hands, by increasing service sector, service will be mainly enjoyed/consumed by the American people, which will not contribute to reducing the national deficits very much, unfortunately.

As a result, manufacturing must be more valuable than service sector with respect to paying off the national debts.

Some American people mentioned that China is functioning as manufacturing hub for US and both parties are benefitting from it. Manufacturing provides jobs such as factory jobs. When the U.S. sent out factories to China, jobs in the U.S. were also lost.
Considering subsistence, jobs are very important even though companies do not make much profits. Theoretically speaking, when manufacturing goes out, people are also free to move which is not true. In reality, only manufacturing goes out and people stay without manufacturing jobs in the U.S. Is this good or bad?
Considering huge amount of cumulative debts with China such as 3.6 trillion $ in the past about thirty years, I have to say that this is bad.
As mentioned in the above, the U.S. has been having trade deficits with China since 1985, that is, for the past thirty years consecutively.
This is a bleeding in human analogy.
Money (Wealth) went out from the U.S. to China consecutively.
In Adam Smith's era, the U.S. has to pay it with gold bullions to China.
Does the U.S. have enough gold bullions to pay to China?
I doubt it.
In other words, the U.S. could have had a serious trouble in paying debts to China for a long time ago if paper money (US$) is linked to gold bullions by 100% which is the case with Adam Smith's era.
How is the U.S. managing it?
Borrowing as economists recommend it, right?
Is this the right way to do it?
Yes, it is as long as the economics theory says.
However, this is only short time relieve, alleviation of symptoms, or postponement of payments. This is not a fundamental cure or solution.
We are now experiencing a huge amount of national debts such as 17.8 trillion dollars in 2014 in total.
By the way, I summed up the U.S. trade deficits with China since 1985 to 2014 and then I got the principal of 3.6 trillion $ in total which represents

about 20% of national debts. In other words, about 20% of the national debts come from the trade deficits with China.

Incidentally, when I consider compound interest rate of using 3% just as an example, I got about 4.6 trillion dollars instead and it represents about 26% of the national debts. In other words, one fourth of the national debts come from the trade deficits with China if I am not mistaken. Actually, ongoing interest rate is 2.5% or less and thus the above calculations are little bid exaggeration in my retro respect. Anyway, we have to do something about it very quickly.

In my opinion, the U.S. needs to stop a bleeding first; otherwise, compound rate of interest will kill you.

(A real cause.)
But why is this happening in the beginning?
Because of the business system we are using based on my observations.
The current business model is a growth model as everyone knows.
As a result, management is required to achieve let's say 6-8% increase on both sales and profits on compound rate basis in every fiscal year.
Let's take 7%, for example, here.
$(1 + 0.07)^5 = 1.40$
Can you see that 7% increase of every year becomes 40% increase in 5 years?
Do you know when I was working for a company of the U.S. subsidiary in Japan, the top management roughly expected us to grow around 10% every year back in 1990s?
$(1+0.10)^5 = 1.61$
Here, it means 60% increase in 5 years.
Everybody knows that in Japan lands are geographically limited and we have severe competitions. In Japan, we do not have much room for expansion, geographically. This is competitive destructions according to Mr. Munger's terminology, right? In my opinion, this kind of expansion model or system is unfit for a confined small market such as Japan.
Do you know why this kind of things happen?
This is because investors or shareholders of companies demand it to the top management of companies.

When the top management failed to achieve this kind of aggressive target/budget, the top management will be fired very quickly, right?
Who demands it?
Investors/shareholders, right?
Why?
By definition in the U.S., "companies are for investors."
Investors have a right to ask for it and we approve it.

Do you know who loses in the end?
In the end, everybody loses. Investors/shareholders lose business and money after torturing employees too much and firing the management more than necessary and thus creating a mess because of too greedy or short-sighted demands/requests. I have seen several US companies withdrew from Japanese market including more than one I worked for.
It took most likely twenty years or more to build business but it took just a few bad decisions to kill the business because of very short sighted short term result oriented decision making or business system.

(Hunter Nature)
Most likely this comes from hunter nature of American business.
As long as we can find large animals to get/catch, we continue to hunt. However, after exhausting large animals, and when we can only find small animals to hunt, we will move on to another new or better field/place for hunting. Looking for efficiency, right?
What will happen when we harvested or exhausted mostly?
This hunting system has a trouble, right?
In history, what comes next?
Shepherds. And after that Agriculture, right?
It means that plowing, planting seeds, waiting to grow, and harvesting.
What is this?
This is basically the same as CIRCULAR ECONOMY which Ms. Ellen MacArthur is talking about according to my understanding.
Can you see the most important concept here?
That is "waiting or patience".

In my opinion, American business model is lacking patience due mainly to very short term orientation of business results such as every quarter.

For example, Mr. B. O. E., ex-IBM vice-president, once told me as follows: "If you want to be a president of US subsidiary in Japan, you have to have serious experiences. You will be judged by every quarter."

I have sensed that I will be fired immediately according to his experiences and hunch.

BY the way, I translated his speech from English to Japanese back in around 1988 in Tokyo, Japan when I was working for a computer software company in Japan. I had no idea about "Token Ring" which he was talking about in his presentation, though.

He is right. I am sure that I will get fired pretty quickly if I am judged by every quarter on the condition that my requirement is something like 10% increase every year.

My point here is that the current growth model is only adequate as long as we have plenty of room for growth and also we have abundant resources.

6. Changed Environments.

<Our Conditions have been changed.>

> However, the situation has been changed and it is crystal clear that we are running out of some of resources shortly such as silver, gold, and indium within 15 years or so, and besides we are currently experiencing the Climate Change right now.
>
> Is consumption driven economic growth model adequate in this circumstances?
>
> I know from psychology that you are blindly following the authority's recommendation or opinion. This is called authority effect in psychology.
>
> If novel laurate economists recommend consumption driven economy, it must be good and no questions asked, right?
>
> But do you know that economists only talk about it from economic point of view? This recommendation come from by looking at a single economic tree point of view instead of looking at entire forests? They are specialists

and they only care about economics or economic prosperity but nothing else.

Now we have dual purposes, which is both economic prosperity and survival or preservation of resources.

From survival point of view, consumption driven economy is totally inadequate and self-killing.

I dare to ask you a question about adequacy of applying the current economics model in this conditions of no abundant resources and clear limitations for growth.

7. Application of Theory.

<The theory is perfect, but the application is wrong.>

In my opinion, the theory itself is perfect as long as we can secure basic assumptions.

Since now the economics theory severely violates the fundamental assumptions, the current economic system is unfit and thus we may want to use better fit models such as conditional free economy and CIRCULAR ECONOMY for adjusting to changing conditions and environments.

OK, let's take an example here.
1. The current economics model is a growth model without limitations.
   In this scenarios, we do not need to have any brake pedal or stopping mechanism, right?
   This is equivalent to blow a balloon and release it in the open air. Which is perfectly fine. There exists no problem in this case.

   (With limitations)
   On the contrary, suppose there exists a limitation for expansion.
   For example, if we are blowing a balloon in a small box, what will happen? What will happen when a balloon reaches to the wall of a small box and starts struggling to find a space to grow or expand? We will have a problem here and everything is not OK, right?

This is similar to our current situation since now we realize that we do not have much room left to grow geographically because we are confined in the frame of the Earth.
Besides, we are running out of resources very shortly which is the case for us within 20 years or so.
In other words, we need to have a brake pedal to slow down (our economic activities) and prepare for stopping when we see a wall in front of the road ahead of us.
Stopping means no growth and thus we are talking about CIRCULAR ECONOMY of Ms. Ellen MacArthur in this case.
Slowing down means a little growth including recession which will be most likely caused by conditional free economy with minimum regulations.
A recession is a lot better than a great depression, though.
If we ignore to take any proactive actions now, a great depression will be inevitable based on my prediction.
By the way, in Japan we experienced a sort of circular economy a long time ago.
In Japan, we closed the door for foreign trades in Tokugawa era, which is around between 1600 A.D. and 1900 A.D.
Economic condition was pretty much circular within Japan and it was not so bad as far as I read it in Japanese history.
In other words, CIRCULAR ECONOMY of Ms. Ellen MacArthur is quite possible or attainable.

Don't you think that our current system of growth model without a brake mechanism is inadequate, antiquated, and obsolete given that our limitations are very clearly visible?

That is why I am proposing a limitation model here which is conditional free economy with minimum regulations.
Conditional means limitations, regulations, and a brake pedal.
In this case, it is free on the condition that it does not hurt the public interests.
The public interests from now on will be preservation of resources and human species, which is our survival.

8. Capitalism, danger of compound rate of interest.

<Danger of Compound Interest Rate >

> Logarithmic increase of Compound Interest Rate.
> As everybody knows what logarithm curve looks like. It looks like J curve, right?
> As time goes by, it gets more and more burdensome and dangerous. When I took a macro-economics class by Dr. Auerbach, he never mentioned about an effect of compound rate of interest, although interest rate itself was considered as a major factor in macro-economics. In reality or the real world, everybody knows that if we borrow money and leave it for thirty years or so, we will have a serious trouble due mainly to compound rate of interest.

9. Application of Free Economy or non-free economy?

> Self-adjusting mechanism only works in free economy when all participants practice it accordingly. In other words, when nobody or no government controls economy and let it be, then self-adjusting mechanism will work.

> When the U.S. had a trade deficit issue with Japan, the U.S. managed it by adjusting exchange rate as far as I know in around 1987 or after.

> I do remember that an American Economist estimated that this issue would be solved at 1$ = 100 YEN while I was studying in the U.S. between 1985 and 1987

> This worked fine although it created a side-effect such as de-valuation of the U.S. $ and thus loosing or weakening buying power of the U.S. $.

> Anyway, exchange rate adjustment worked fine based on Japanese example although this is equivalent to selling yourself short or cheap in business context.

> The U.S. has not done the same with China as far as I know.

China may be too big or too strong or whatever the reason may be. One of the reasons may be China's function as a manufacturing hub for the U.S. When Chinese Yuan gets stronger, the prices of the U.S. products manufactured in China also go up and thus those products will lose a price competitive edge also.

Do you see that? This is my whole point of self-adjusting mechanism here. Since the U.S earth companies get hurt with this, these companies have to do something else. If these companies find another country as a manufacturing hub, the same cycle repeats. In other words, the U.S. lose wealth in the end by devaluation of the U.S. dollars. Or these companies will give up an idea of manufacturing hub and productions will go back to the original state which is manufacturing in the U.S. When these companies start manufacturing in the U.S. again, everything will go back to normal. When Production goes up, Employment also goes up and Income goes up, which is not true in the U.S. right now unfortunately. You see, self-adjusting mechanism will work like this.

Besides, fundamentally China uses controlled economy which is totally different from free economy from the beginning. China comes from communism and opened its market in 1978. I tend to believe that China says that it takes time to adjust to free economy system. But about 35 years of adjusting period is long enough. Now China's GDP is the second biggest in the world after that of the U.S.'.

<China's Case.>

China's impact on free economy is getting more and more significant these days and thus self-adjusting mechanism of free economy is getting more and more paralyzed these days accordingly based on my observations.
Cocoon period for China is already over.
Just in case, China does not accept free fluctuations of exchange rate, the U.S. could levy import duties on all Chinese goods except basic foods as a substitution for exchange rate adjustment. Although this practice may

infringe WTO (World Trade Organization)'s agreement, China is infringing concept and practices of free economy anyway by controlling free fluctuations of exchange rate as far as I see it.

Exchange rate adjustments and imposing import duties on all goods will work the same as an end effect. Considering Engel's Law or Engel's co-efficient, duties on basic foods should be excluded since it will hurt low-income households more severely than rich people.

Engel's Law or co-efficient means as follows:

Proportion of income spent on foods decreases as income increases. The poorer the household, the larger the percentage of spending on foods in total spending. In other words, poor people spend larger portion of their income on foods than rich people. On the contrary, rich people's expenditures on foods consist only small percentage of their total income.

10. Free fluctuations of Exchange rate.

Exchange Rate / at 1 US dollar = x Chinese yuan

1980 1.4984
1985 2.9367
1986 3.4528
1989 3.7651
1990 4.7832
1991 5.3234
1994 8.6187

<Exchange Rate between US$ and Chinese Yuan>

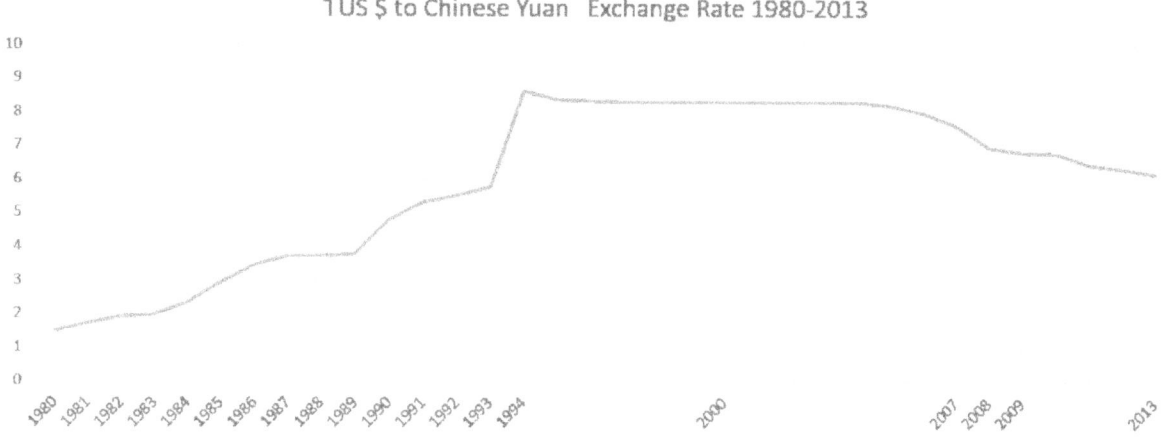

(Graph 8, Exchange rate between the U.S. $ and Chinese Yuan. Data Source: Wiki Exchange Rates, etc.)

> Note: The above graph does not make sense at all from free economy point of view. Chinese Yuan had been getting weaker with the U.S. dollar until 1994 while the U.S. trade deficits with China had also been increased, which is contradictory. Anyway, the above movements are very strange and thus somebody must be manipulating it, most likely Chinese government.
> It is very clear that self-adjusting mechanism is being paralyzed based on the strange movement of exchange rate between the two countries.

11. Examples.

<Leeman Case in 2008 and my personal experience.>

<My Personal Case>

> I lost about 95% of my deposit on golf membership in Japan. This golf club filed bankruptcy or revitalizing plan to the Tokyo court, which was accepted as usual. I received a legal letter from a lawyer/revitalizer/trustee that 95% of my deposit is cancelled and it will pay me 5% of my deposit on installment basis something like in 5 years or so. What can I say or do other than

accepting it? It is too late to do anything after bankruptcy claim was filed and accepted by the court in my understanding.

Anyway, I lost my money because this entity filed bankruptcy code.

When this kind of thing happens, my spending will shrink because less money is now available or I got poorer by losing money.

<Leeman Case>

The same thing with the Leeman case in 2008.

When a large company such as Leeman went to bankrupt, it could incur chain reactions of bankruptcies of many companies involved, which had some business with Leeman. Lots of companies and people lost money but at least they could borrow money from banks underneath of FRB because of increased money supply thanks to FRB by lending money from borrowing in a way of issuing the U.S. treasury bonds, etc. if I am not mistaken. In other words, people or companies involved lost lots of money and/but financed its loss by the governmental borrowing, I guess. Actually I honestly do not know what kind of deals were made or done at that time.

Government-FRB supplied enough money to the market (companies/people) through banks underneath with the money by the governmental borrowing.

The U.S. market absorbed huge amount of money.

1. Actually consumers already spent huge amounts of money in advance with bad loans.
2. As a result, companies and people involved lost lots of money because of bankruptcy/defaults.
3. The Government supported enough money by borrowing. The Government loses interest payments. The Government increased national debts.

Did you see the real cause here?

<Real causes>

A. Both consumption driven economy and cruel business system are real causes of it in my opinion.

1. People bought new cars and built new houses on credit or borrowed money (Bad Loans). (People spent money first)
2. Leeman lent it or accepted bad loans but Leeman went to bankrupt. Huge amounts of bad loans became as real losses and payment became due. Obviously most borrowers cannot pay for it and a disaster would happen or financial market would corrupt accordingly if nothing were done. Here a saver showed up, namely the U.S. government/FRB of course.
3. Money supply was increased and thus the U.S. governmental debt was increased accordingly.

In other words, people spent money first and the U.S. government financed it by borrowing later/afterwards in order to avoid an economic contraction, recession, or disaster.
If I make it simple, this is the same as below stated in reverse order:

<What Happened in Reversed Order. >

1. The government provided money without much choice.
2. Leeman cheated and went to bankrupt.
3. Some consumers cheated and over-spent money without being able to pay for it (bad loans.)

(In the end, Government=Public paid for it.)
In the end, the government took care of bad guys' bad behaviors.
The public supported over spenders and cheaters by the name of consumption driven economy proposed by economists. Over spenders and cheaters will prevail in this system, unfortunately. We need to change the whole system. The same system, the same result.
Since we also need to change our habits, I am proposing Benjamin Franklin campaign. Temperance, thrift, and industry.

What is the problem?
There are at least two issues here.

1. Compound rate of interest.
2. Borrowing money from outside of the U.S.

With current amounts of national debts such as $18 trillion, interest payment alone amounts to about $0.43 trillion. Compound rate of interest will place a significant burden on a borrower which is the U.S. government.

In economics theory of a confined environment, both lenders and borrowers exist/stay in the same economic unit. In this case, lenders are both the U.S. citizens and the U.S. corporations, and the borrower is the U.S. government.

Can you see that lenders and borrowers are ultimately the same in this case? The U.S. citizens and the U.S. corporations own the U.S. government, right?

When the U.S. government goes on default, the debts will be absorbed by the U.S. citizens and the U.S. corporations and this deal is kind of fair because this is kind of cancelling out the debts each other in the U.S. or within the economic unit.

Did you notice that lenders are affluent people those who have extra money to lend? When the U.S. government goes on default, most likely rich people those who are creditors of lending money cannot get their money back and thus lose their lending money. This works like re-distribution of income such as from the rich to the poor in the U.S. This only changes distribution of debt burden from the public to the Haves. In other words, this only changes proportion of the debts among its participants.

This will work fine or great for making Gini statistics more favorable in the U.S. in my opinion. Most likely this is a self-adjusting mechanism called by Adam Smith or economists in a confined market or a single country economics model. This may be the reason why economists always say that everything will be fine, everything will be taken care of in the end according to the theory which is not fit right now.

Taking a look at situation so far in the U.S., Gini statistics' situation is getting worse and worse these days. In other words, rich people get richer and richer while poor people get poorer and poorer these days. This is a reflection of monopolistic conditions in the market since very few companies or individuals make huge money while the rests either go broke or get bought/acquired.

<The economics theory is not working as intended right now.>

(A basic assumption of a confined market is not met now.)

In the current real world, economy is malfunctioning.

Everybody knows that the U.S. treasury bonds are also purchased by foreigners such as foreign governments because of global nature of economy now.

When the U.S. government goes on default, lots of lenders are foreign governments and thus self-adjusting mechanism will not work as beautiful as the above mentioned case and thus this is not fair anymore.

If we want to apply economics theory while keeping its assumptions, we have to apply it on the Earth basis. We need to have the Earth Government accordingly.

In this case, the U.S. situation will be similar to that of Greece in EC/EU.

The Earth government will command payment of debts to the U.S. first before lending more money further, for example.

Our economic system worked great for the past about 70 years or so after the WWII because the system was well fit for the circumstances and conditions at that time.

Since our conditions and circumstances have been completely changed, it is time for us to change our systems entirely because our current system does not fit well for the current conditions such that there exit limitations. We can clearly foresee the shortage of resources and a clear sign of limitation for growth.

Do you think that does our current system satisfy our current public interests? Given shortage of natural resources, is it logical to facilitate consumption and use up resources as efficiently and fast as possible?
Right now we are using consumption driven economics model which is most efficient for deprivation of natural resources.
This is analogous to a relay of 100 meter dash race.

In my opinion, it is time to change from 100 meter dash to jogging and walking eventually. In other words, we may want to slow down our economic activities gradually to save time and resources until we come up with better systems or solutions.
Up to now, our best solution may be "CIRCULAR ECONOMY".

<The U.S. National Debts>
17,824,071,380.82 (9/30/2014)

10,024,724,896,912.49 (9/30/2008)
9,007,653,372,262.48 (9/30/2007)

(Graph 9, the U.S. national debts 2007 V.S. 2014.)

(Data Source: Treasury Direct, historical debt outstanding.)

    The U.S. debts got almost doubled in seven years in the past from 2007 to 2014.
This seems something to do with money supply expansion after 2007/2008 financial crisis in the U.S.

This is nothing wrong in itself and this is just a tip of an iceberg in my opinion. Real issues here is that we are using an inadequate or unfit economics model for the current circumstances such as limited resources and limited room for growth.

My points are as follows:
<Consumption driven economy is no longer fit.>
Consumption driven economy makes sense when we have abundant resources and no limitations for growth.
However, since it is crystal clear that some resources are running out in the near future and thus we see a clear limitation for growth considering diminishing rate of return theory also.
Consumption driven economy is no longer fit or justifiable.

<Our Current business model for efficiency is also unfit.>
Besides, our ever growing cruel business model is also causing some issues in my opinion.
For example, current business model is a model looking for efficiency. It commands high rate of sales growth and ROE (return on investment).
What will happen if we push too hard?
People start cheating based on the past observations, right?
Why?
Because we are commanding impossible things to achieve.
Although there is not much room to grow, our system commands compound rate of high growth and thus everybody starts struggling.
In this kind of situation, we have basically only two choices.

Eat or get eaten. Kill or get killed. One of our basic needs for survival is being threatened. When our basic needs are threatened, people think and act illogically. In other words, it will cause cheating

Our animal nature for survival will show up and we do not get killed so easily. Before getting killed or eaten, lots of people, not all of us, though, start cheating.

This is happening in the business world right now in my opinion.

By the way, I saw lots of cheating personally in business, although I was not directly involved in it very fortunately.

I heard that one of our salesmen shipped goods at intentionally wrong address before closing date of a fiscal year when I was working for a company of the U.S. subsidiary in Japan.

The shipment got returned of course some days later but it was after the fiscal year or in a new fiscal year. Therefore, he made his budget in this fiscal year but he started from negative figures/sales in the next fiscal year. At least he made his budget this year; otherwise, he will be punished or let go very shortly! I knew a sales manager Mr. M. of age around 60 years old, a former head of sales department of that company. He told me that every month he called up a couple of the worst performers from the bottom and gave them one month to improve their sales performances. If they did not improve their sales results in the next month, he told them to go to find another job somewhere. He told me that he will not die peacefully because of that. Actually I agree with him.

Do you know that I was assigned to be a person in charge for seeing him off when he retired? In Japan usually lots of his former subordinates come to say good bye to a retiring person like him. I tell you nobody came as far as I saw other than me when he left his office on the last day. He left his office very quietly alone for good. Actually he treated me well. He told his stories how to manage sales, etc. over lunches and coffees for several times. He is a nice person in normal situation but he is mean when his job is at risk, which is very normal and thus I do not blame on him.

You know these things better than I do because people get fired more often in the U.S.

<This is another cheating story.>

Both a sales manager and a marketing manager collaborated making sales budget by shipping huge amount of goods to a newly borrowed warehouse and reported it as a sales before the end of fiscal year. Do you know what will happen when we find this kind of thing? Be quiet, say nothing, and no questions asked, right? Mind our own business only, right?
Why do I know it? I know this marketing manager very well and we went for drinking often. While we were drinking he told me this story, which every manager knows as far as I can think of.
Do you know what I did? Nothing, of course. Why should I? This is none of my business. Besides, stories over drinking is considered as off-records in Japan. Stay away from danger from my point of view.

I also read some cheating stories in accounting, etc. in the US.
My point here is that this is just a tip of an iceberg.
In other words, people are struggling in a no way out situation under the current growth system and people will not die so quietly or easily when our jobs are being at risk. Lots of people will try cheating before getting fired or finished.
Yes, this is a sign of danger for us.
Is current system really best fit for us?

(A real cause of cheating.)
These cheating stories go on and on.
Why is that?
Aren't we doing impossible thing because of the unfit system?
My father once told me that aren't you doing impossible thing when I lost my health.
I knew I was doing impossible thing. Since it is the system and it is the way it is, what else can I do?
But now I can clearly explain it logically that what we are doing under the current system does not satisfy our public interest of our survival such as preserving resources and saving lives of our future generations.

We need to change the current systems and change our life styles also in response to changed and further changing environments. This is logical thing to do for us, isn't it?

<Detail Analysis of Money Supply Expansion.>

<2007/2008 financial crisis in the U.S.>

After the incidence of financial crisis in 2007/2008, the U.S. expanded money supply in order to avoid a contraction, recession, or disaster.
There must have had no other way; however, this is just an alleviation of symptoms and this is not a fundamental cure, which will be explained as follows:

<Analysis>

1. Money Supply Increase/expansion.
    A. Money supply M1 was increased by 117% from 2008 to 2015.
    B. Money Supply M2 was increased by 57% from 2008 to 2015.
       (Where M1 is cash equivalent. M2 is M1 plus bank deposit equivalent.)

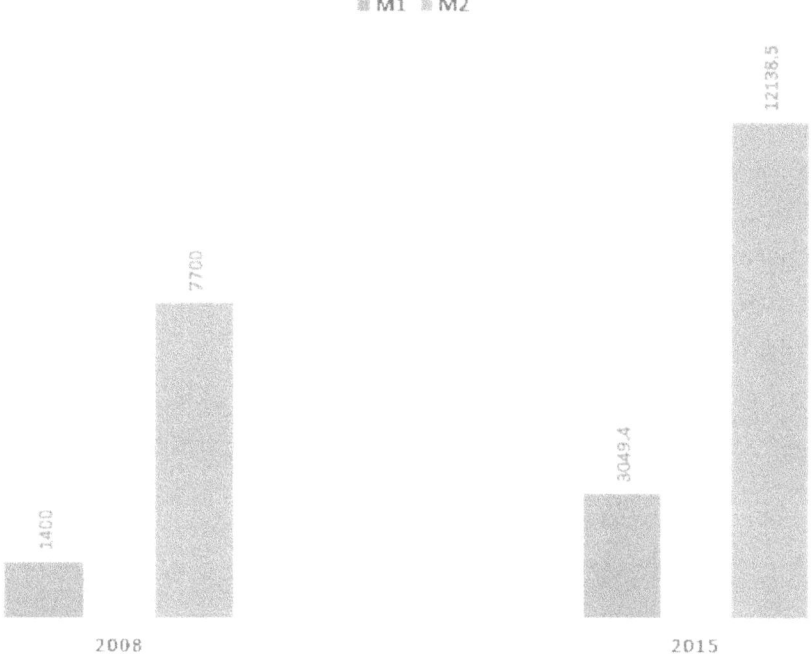

(Graph 10, M1 and M2. Data Source: Tradingeconomics.com.)

Both M1 and M2 went up after 2007/2008 financial crisis.

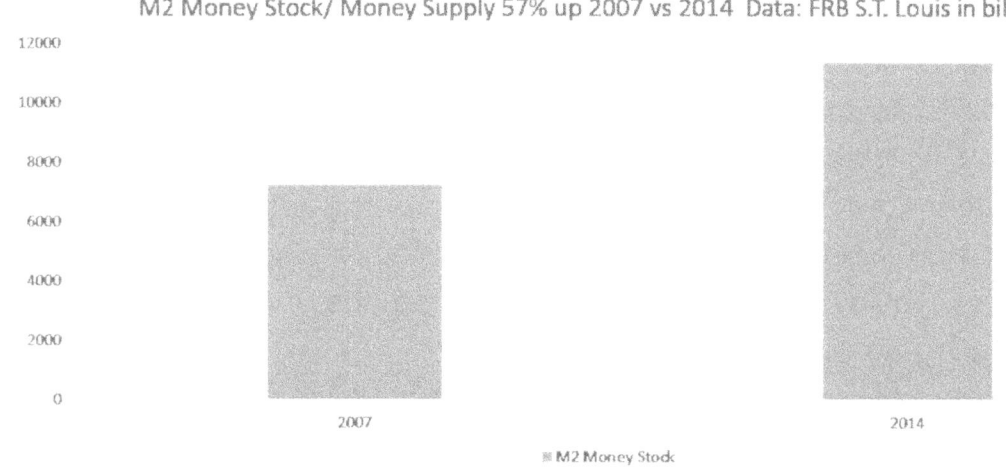

(Graph 11, M2 2007 V.S. 2014. Data Source: FRB S.T. Louis.)

Note: M2 must be more appropriate here because it includes banking accounts, which strongly affect spending propensity according to my understanding.

<Temporary Fix>

(Blood transfusion)
In human analogy M2 is equivalent to blood in our body in my opinion.
In other words, increase of M2 is equivalent to blood transfusion when emergency situation.
However, this is just a temporary or quick fix which will not last very long, which is the same as blood transfusion. We cannot keep implementing blood transfusion for too long.

<Detailed Descriptions>

When investors and lenders of money/bad loans realize loss on lending, they inevitably try to withdraw or get back their lending money as quickly as possible. Financial market will become panic or crush if this situation is untreated.

(Overspending beyond their means)
What really happened is that new houses were already built and sold and new cars were already sold/purchased beyond their means, affordability, or life style constraints/limitations. These people spent more than they could afford or overspent, which is cheating in my opinion.
Prices of houses went down and loan payments started being defaulted and a number of financial institutions went to bankrupts accordingly. Financial institutions should have never made bad loans in the beginning, which is also cheating in my opinion.
In the end, those used houses were left and those used cars were left there as a result. These were unnecessary from the beginning, which is oversupply considering supply/demand function and thus losses of both money and natural resources. Lenders lost money. Innocent people were also included

in lenders those who bought financial securities from financial institutions without knowing about bad loans because the information was beautifully hidden in a high-tech way.

In this case, actually lenders have ownership of these second-hand houses and used cars when loans are defaulted. I do not know how much losses it created but it must be lots of money because houses and cars are no longer new and de-valued and it costs money to sell them. When lots of used houses and used cars are being on sale, prices will go down very steeply because of demand and supply function.

Who are the losers?
Obviously lenders lost money very substantially when financial institutions went to bankrupts.
By the way, main job of financial institutions are both borrowing money and lending money in order to make profits between the two.
By lending money when it got defaulted, financial institutions get hurt first. Who will get hurt next? Those who are involved with financial institutions such as customers, depositors (us), companies, and the U.S. government. This is terrible.

Who are the gainers?
In my opinion, nobody.
This is called a short-term gain and a long-term pain based on Mr. Brian Tracy's phrase.
Over spenders such as Buyers of new houses and new cars gained utility for using it for a while but eventually they lost it all. Since lots of these people have some faults by borrowing money beyond their means, I do not feel sorry for them, not all of them, though.
However, innocent people also got involved and lost money when financial institutions went to bankrupts.
If somebody has a deposit or saving account at those institutions, what will happen when those went to bankrupts?
Most likely these lenders/customers must have lost substantial portion of their lending, although I do not know what really happened to them.

Anyway, the real cause is overspending beyond their means/income which was encouraged/facilitated by our current consumption driven economy and business model.

So what are real problems?
1. Current business model of over-facilitation of spending.
2. Too high Life Style with respect to income status. Or over-spending habits beyond its income/means.

(Comparison to Benjamin Franklin.)

This must be a sure way of ruining our lives and country when comparing them to Benjamin Franklins' 13 virtues as follows:

Due mainly to copy right issue, I am talking about only 3 virtues here.
1. Temperance. "Eat not to Dulness. Drink not to Elevation."
2. Frugality.
3. Industry.

"Virtues; Frugality and Industry, by freeing me from my remaining Debt, and producing Affluence and Independence----." ("The autobiography of Benjamin Franklin")

As far as I know, he is one of the fathers of the United States. He lived with these virtues and he became successful and wealthy, I suppose.

Can you see the difference between the two?
1. All you can eat and drink V.S. Eat and drink moderately.
2. Consumption driven economy V.S. Frugality.
3. Many holidays and working less. V.S. Industry.

<Results>

Financial crisis and huge debts. V.S. Success and Wealth.

Which is right, economists or Benjamin Franklin?

It is clear that Benjamin Franklin is right based on the results of above mentioned.

Economists fostered accumulation of debts by consumption driven economy instead of accumulating wealth of the U.S.

I tend to believe that economists are irresponsible because of including an option of default in the worst case. Real life is different from a game or theory. If it is a game, it is fine to start over a new game again by going to default. In the real life, when the U.S. goes on default, it will create most likely another depression which will last for years and thus lots of people may go starvation. In other words, we experience pains in the real world where no pain is considered in theory.

What economists are recommending us is that spend now as much as possible and pay it later as late as possible in order to maximize our current economic well-being or prosperity at the expense of that of future generations'.

They will lead us to a disaster in the end or in the coming future.

Yes, we enjoyed economic prosperity for the past 60 years or so at the expense of what?

There always exists cycle of production and consumption.

We cannot keep spending forever.

We cannot keep increasing borrowing forever.

Economists only delayed payments. Postponed payments. The due will come in the end or not so far away.

Let's listen what Benjamin Franklin says.

<Temperance>

Temperance. Change our habits. Change our eating habits. We are consuming too much. We are eating too much. Let's abandon consumption-driven economy, which is now more harmful than beneficial. Consumption driven economy does not make sense at all for the betterment of the country right now. We can no longer afford consumption driven economy since our conditions have been changed.

<Frugality>

Frugality. Stop spending too much. Live within our means. Do not waste resources.

Industry. Increase productive labor. Stop taking too many holidays, which are unproductive. We should be working more or increase productive labor instead of increasing holidays, unproductive labor.

Does our current business model meet the public interests?
What are the public interests right now? We are facing a semi-emergency situations now. We are facing the Climate Change, shortage of natural resources, and not enough room for expansion.
Do we have to consume or spend as much as and as quickly as possible? This is like we are having a competition of the fastest and biggest eater now while foods are getting short in predictable period of time, for example.
We are spending and consuming as much as possible under the current economic and business systems.
To make matters worse, economists and the U.S. Government recommend and facilitate consumer spending in order to improve economy while sacrificing our survival needs. Current economic system is forever growth and forever expansion model because its assumptions are no limitations, abundant resources, etc., which are not true anymore.
Aren't we a little illogical?
While clearly knowing limitations and shortages, we are still assuming no limitations and abundant resources?
It seems to me that this is illogical, insane, and self-killing.

Chapter 4. Dysfunctional economics theory.
<How Consumption driven economy works?>

Based on my understandings, consumption driven economy works as follows:

1. Consumption first. When we consume more, demand goes up. Here we are talking about demand/supply curve. When Demand goes up, Supply goes up. When Supply goes up Employment goes up. When company/factory produce more, additional work is created and Employment goes up and thus Income goes up. What is the basic assumptions in this economic model? This is a single nation model and thus all of Consumption, Demand, Supply, Employment, and Income are confined in a single country.
In other words, Consumption creates Demand in the U.S. When Demand goes up in the U.S., Supply goes up in the U.S. When Supply goes up in the U.S., Employment goes up in the U.S. and thus Income goes up in the U.S. When American people consume more, American people need to produce more and thus America people work more and make more Income. This is great, right? This scenario only works as long as the basic assumptions are met; namely, everything must occur in a confined market or in the U.S.

2. <Violation of basic assumptions.>
(The theory does not fit or application is wrong.)
(Economy is dysfunctional within a range of the U.S.)
In reality, since economy is global now, consumption driven economy works as follows:
Consumption in the U.S. creates Demand. When Demand goes up in the U.S., Supply from China (Production in China) goes up, for example. Since China is manufacturing hub for the U.S., right? When Supply from China goes up, Employment and Income goes up in China where actual manufacturing is taken place. In this case both Employment and Income in the U.S. may or may not go up proportionately because Production is not conducted very much in the U.S. anymore. While American people consume more, American people do not work more (at factory) and do not make more money. Instead, Chinese people work more (at factory) and make more money/income. Do you know that the U.S. has been having

trade deficits with China for the past 30 years or so since 1985, and the amounts of the trade deficits are about $3.6 trillion?

This is also consistent with the data I have as follows:

The U.S. household income is not growing very much these days.

China's GDP or what China produce is growing very rapidly considering that China has become the second biggest economy in the world now. Chinese people are getting richer and richer as long as I know.

And then how the U.S. is managing the situation?

How is it possible to keep growing or managing its economy? Borrowing money, right?

Do you realize that borrowing only works well in a confined market such as within the U.S?

When the U.S. government borrows money within the U.S. and when the government goes on default, it is fine. Why? Because lenders and a borrower are ultimately the same. The U.S. citizens own the U.S. government. Borrowed money by government was used for the public purpose and thus this is basically the same as public spending financed by tax. When the U.S. government goes on default, it will work like re-distribution of negative income or charging expenses afterwards. This will only change the proportion of the burden from the public to actual lenders. All money stay in the U.S. including interest payments.

However, this is not the case right now since economy is global.

When the U.S. government borrows money by issuing treasury bonds, many foreign governments purchase these.

All money does not stay in the U.S. Some of Interest payments will go out from the U.S. or gained by foreign governments/foreigners at least.

When the U.S. government goes on default, lenders and borrowers are not necessarily the same in this case. Lenders may ask for a collateral in this case, for example.

Major Foreign Holders of Treasury Securities (in billions of dollars)

	Aug 2015
China, Mainland	1270.5
Japan	1197.0
Carib Bkg Ctrs 4/	329.0

Oil Exporters 3/   293.2
Brazil   255.3

Total   6098.7(About $6 trillion)
(Data: treasury.gov)
(Note: Carib Bkg Ctrs 4 could be the U.S. fund money at tax heavens and thus this could be included as domestic but I leave it as it is.)

Note) The U.S. national debts are about $18 trillion dollars in 2015.
6/18= about a third of the U.S. borrowing are from foreign governments.
In other words, about one third of $0.43 trillion of interest payment ($0.14 trillion) goes out from the U.S. to abroad every year, which is a bleeding in human analogy.

You see that this is a danger of ignoring basic assumptions but yet use economics theory blindly as if it works perfectly fine. Is this logical thing to do?

  A. Basic rule of thumb is as follows:
When we consume more, we need to work more and make more income. There always exists a cycle of production (+) and consumption (-). Work (+) and spending (-).
In other words, when we consume more (-), it creates us more work (+) and thus it makes us busier and leaves less time for leisure or idleness basically.
On the contrary, in the U.S., people consumer more and more (-) and yet take more and more holidays, which is unproductive labor (0). "People work less when country gets rich", according to Dr. Auerbach. This was a paradox for me when I took a macro-economic class by Dr. Auerbach at UCR. I finally got you. Economists are not magicians. Borrowing is not a panacea. Borrowing is just a quick fix instead of a permanent solution. Economists only postponed payments. Now what? We need to start paying for it and it is kind of painful in my opinion. This cannot be done under democracy based on the past experiences. "Budget didn't work for the government" according to Dr. Auerbach. Budget will never work

for the government under democracy in my opinion. Therefore, I am proposing conditional democracy here. We use democracy on the condition that it does not hurt the public interests. The public here refers to people on earth instead of just American people. If the U.S. goes on defaults, it will create a disaster such as another world depression inevitably. We need to create an Earth Government for all people on earth and may want to take some burdens off from the U.S. government. The public interests in this case are as follows:

1. Avoid a disaster such as another great depression.

    How?

    1. Make our ends meet. Stop bleeding. Make the trade balance break-even or positive. Make the trade balance break-even between the U.S. and China to begin with.
    2. Cut the national debts. Work more and spend less.
        I recommend Benjamin Franklin Campaign.
        Temperance, Frugality, Industry, etc.
        Change couch-potatoes into Benjamin Franklin, Jr.
        Abandon consumption driven economy.
        Apply industry driven economy instead.

    3. <Benjamin Franklin Campaign.>
        While I was reading Benjamin Franklin's autobiography, it seemed that economists have been ruining and weakening the U.S. by spoiling the U.S. public through consumption driven economy, etc.
        Benjamin Franklin lived with 13 virtues which led him to his success. Many American citizens are living totally different from the 13 virtues, especially with respect to temperance, thrift, and industry.
        Based on my observations, American citizens are led to spenders, holiday enjoyers. We are talking about quality of life here, right? Yes, but we went to too far based on our results so far. We are acting and behaving anti-thrift and anti-industry for the past 60 years or so. In addition, considering all you can eat and drink system, which leads to anti-temperance. In other words, American citizens are completely against Benjamin Franklin's success formula. "When country gets rich, people work less." No wonder why the U.S. has been losing wealth for

the past 60 years or so. People are eating up wealth created by ancestors instead of creating wealth for new generations.

I know that most successful, affluent people have similar virtues to those of Benjamin Franklin's, especially with respect to temperance, thrift, and industry.

The country is not an exception.

The country is just an aggregate of individuals and thus the country's performance such as GDP (what we produce) depends on performance of individuals as a whole, obviously.

Lots of people in the U.S. are spoiled by consumption driven economy and thus lots of people acquired very bad habits such as overspending, work less and less, and eat more & drink more, which are hard to get rid of.

We should follow Benjamin Franklin's success formula or 13 virtues.

Abandon Consumption driven economy and we should live by the equivalent of 13 virtues from now on.

Since we have already spent it or consumed it by borrowing, we need to produce and pay for it from now on.

Although it may take 4700 years to pay it back, we still need to do it.

Like Mr. Brian Tracy says, "failure is not an option".

By the same token, default is not an option for the U.S.

In other words, it is fine to take your time but the failure is not an option.

<Habits and traits of successful people.>
BY the way, I have never seen successful American people who are not hard workers.

As far as I witnessed American Top executives, they work very hard and long hours and most of them work a half day in the morning on Saturdays. This is the success model or role model as an individual in my opinion.

<Lots of people have bad habits.>
On the other hand, probably lots of American people try to work as less as possible and at the same time spend as much as possible, which is similar to that of Roman Empire's citizens. Because a majority counts in democracy system, when life styles of underachievers' become dominant,

the country will become less productive and less competitive as a whole and thus GDP will suffer in the end.

<Pit fall of democracy>
This is also very dangerous because a majority of opinion and habits/life styles determine decisions of the country under democracy.
Since nobody wants to take pains, painful conduct will never be accomplished under democracy such as cutting the national debts as quickly as possible.
As you can see from the above stated, we need something new such as an Earth Government from now on in order to accomplish something necessary but painful deeds. The earth government can exercise sort of conditional democracy for the public interests. The Earth Government can strongly request cutting the national debts of the U.S. on the condition that it contributes the public interest of the whole world, for example. Or the earth government can strongly request China to let the exchange rates fluctuate freely without intervention.

4. <Recovery after 2007/2008 Financial crisis.>

   (The Same System, the Same Result.)

Nothing seems to be changed after the crisis as far as I analyzed the situation. Only the national debts seem to be increased because of money supply expansion in the U.S. In other words, money supply expansion was just an alleviation of symptoms and thus it was not a fundamental cure at all. The same system or process, the same result. Spending more and working less creates always more debts fundamentally.
We need fundamental cures. Fundamental cures must be that changing our current economic model as well as business model in addition to life style changes including habits change from spending to saving. In other words, we may want to choose a role model of successful people instead of that of unsuccessful people as a whole in the U.S. We need to change couch-potatoes into Benjamin Franklin, Jr. Working hard, working longer hours, and thrift should be a role model for all of us to follow in my opinion.

We will not get a result as quickly as we wish based on my experiences. Although I started following Benjamin Franklin's virtues, nothing seems to happen to me so far. Most likely it may take decades until I see some visible improvements. However, it will be a matter of time since the direction is right. Once I made the virtues into my habits, it would become automatic and it would no longer take any efforts to keep it.

<Analysis>

1. Dow Jones in US$ went up by 38% from 2007 to 2015 and by 115% from 2009 to 2015.

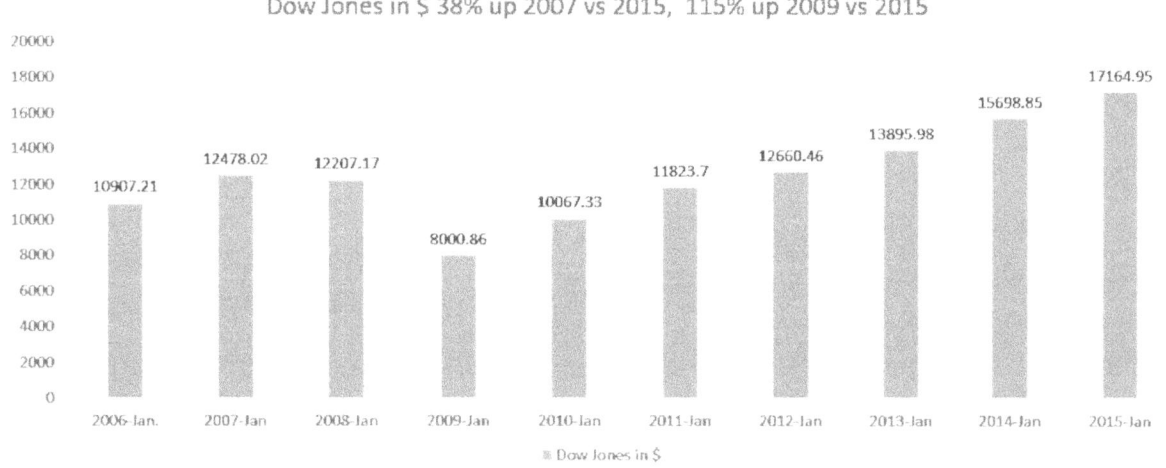

(Graph 12, Dow Jones. Data Source: I got it from internet. You can find it very easily and take a look at on internet. Please just look at a trend of the above graph.)

Note: This might be just swelling or bloating effect of money supply expansion based on my observations.

This looks successful and everybody is looking at and talking about these figures, right?

Yes, Dow Jones went up but what is the side effect?

The side effect is an increase of the national debts as well as interest payments as follows:

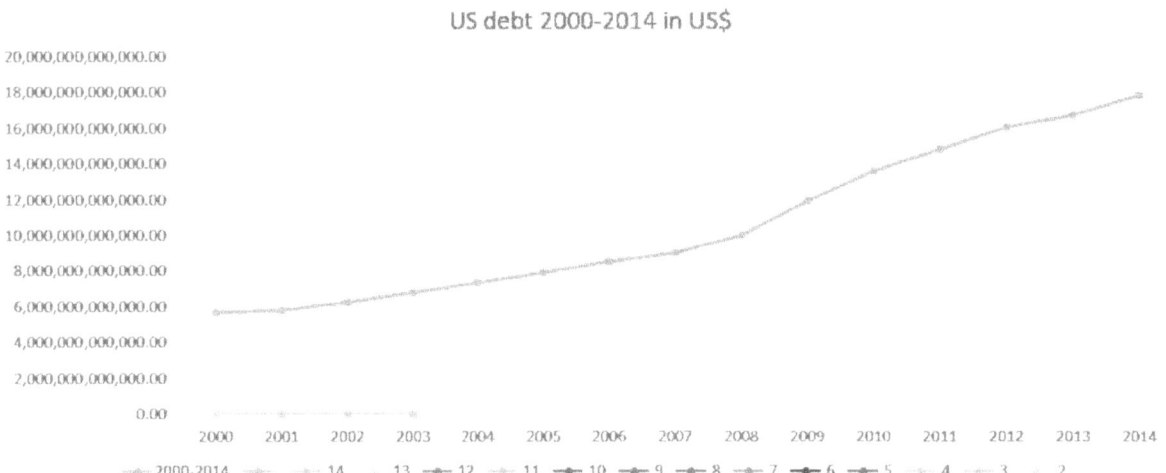

(Graph 13, the U.S. national debts. Data Source: Treasury Direct.)

Can you see that the U.S. national debts have been accelerated from around 2008 when financial crisis happened?

Upward trend of Dow Jones and that of National Debt looks similar, right? Although I do not have access to a correlation analysis software, it looks fairly obvious that the above two must have a strong correlation by taking a look at the above two graphs.

Since money expansion was financed by the national debts, these two must have a strong correlation.

Besides when more money comes in to financial markets, demand for stocks increases. Given availability of stocks stay the same, increased demand by overflow of money will push up stock prices because of more/increased competition for purchasing.

In other words, this is just an effect of swelling or bloating caused by money supply expansion because of avalanches of money inflow into stock markets.

<Alleviation of Symptoms.>

Anyway, the United States succeeded to alleviate 2007/2008 financial crises without fundamental cures in my opinion. In other words, another financial crisis will come in the near future. It is just a matter of time since the real causes have not been treated yet.

What will happen when the United States encounters another financial crisis?

Doing the same thing by borrowing money, right?

I am not so sure whether the United States will be able to afford it or not at the next time.

We have to treat the real causes ASAP.

<Interest Payments>

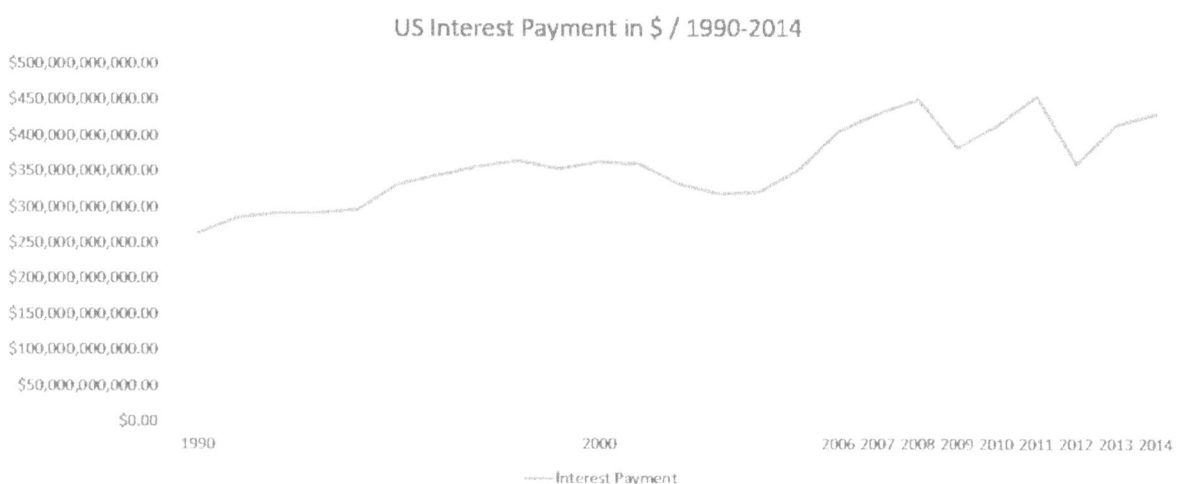

(Graph14, interest payments. Data Source: treasurydirect.gov)

This graph shows a trend of interest payments.

In 2014, 0.43 trillion $ of interest payments.

This is a serious issue in my opinion.

Interest payments went up from around 2006/2007.

This looks not so threatening at first glance.

However, considering compound rate of interest and amounts of the national debts, any financial analysts will start sweating for sure. If not, I will ask for their qualifications personally.

Roughly speaking, this is about $60,000 of debt per capita and $1,400 of interest payment annually. This is equivalent to the average annual median household income in the U.S. If you leave it untreated or unpaid for about 25 years, this amount will get doubled based on a 3% compound rate of interest. $(1.03)^{25} = 2.09$ These amounts will become about two years of average annual household income, which will be very hard to pay it back.

Do you think that you will be able to afford additional loans or debts when the second blow or financial crisis occur in the future?

<Diagnosis. What is the issue?>

<GDP>

(Graph 15, GDP. Data Source: Bureaus of Economic Analysis.)

Actually when I learned from Dr. Auerbach, he used GNP, Gross National Product, which is what we produce. In other words, whether it is GDP or GNP, I mean it what we produce in this book, sorry.

The above graph shows GDP, Gross Domestic Product, and thus equivalent to what we produce in the United States.

GDP is growing steadily.

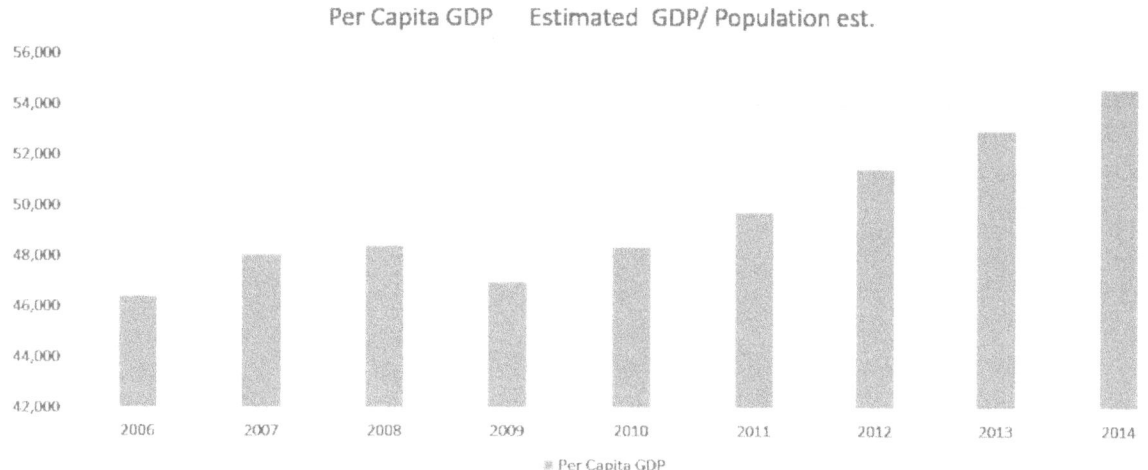

(Graph 16, Per Capita GDP. GDP / # of Populations.)

Per Capita GDP is also growing.
So far so good.

<Dow Jones>

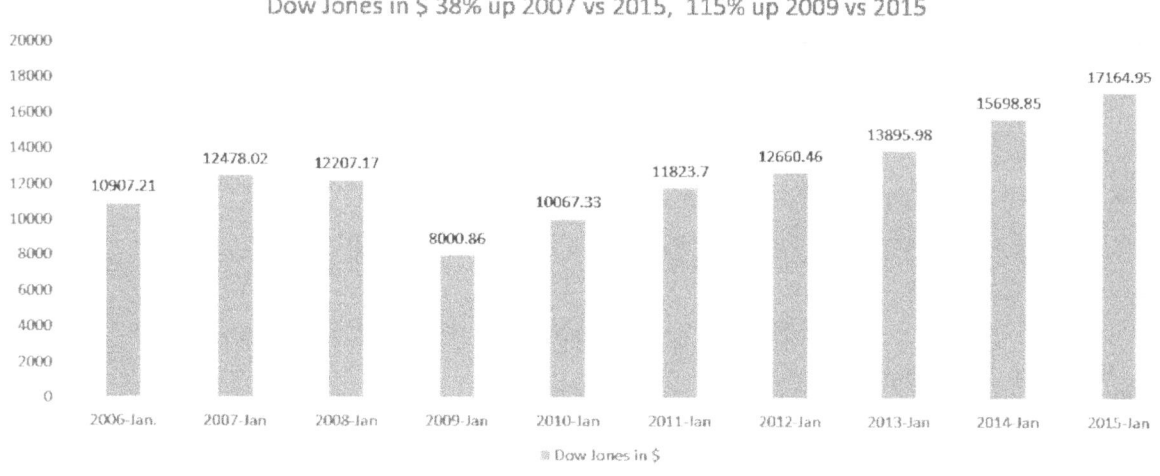

(Graph 17, Dow Jones.)

Dow Jones went down sharply from 2008 to 2009, which was the impact of financial crisis.

This is an indication of performance in financial markets, right?
Dow Jones industrial average is growing steadily. So far so good.
Everybody talks about the above two, right?
I have a very strong concern about this increasing trend considering expansion of money supply effect. This could be just an effect of swelling or bloating caused by massive money supply expansion since 2007/2008.

<Trade Balance>

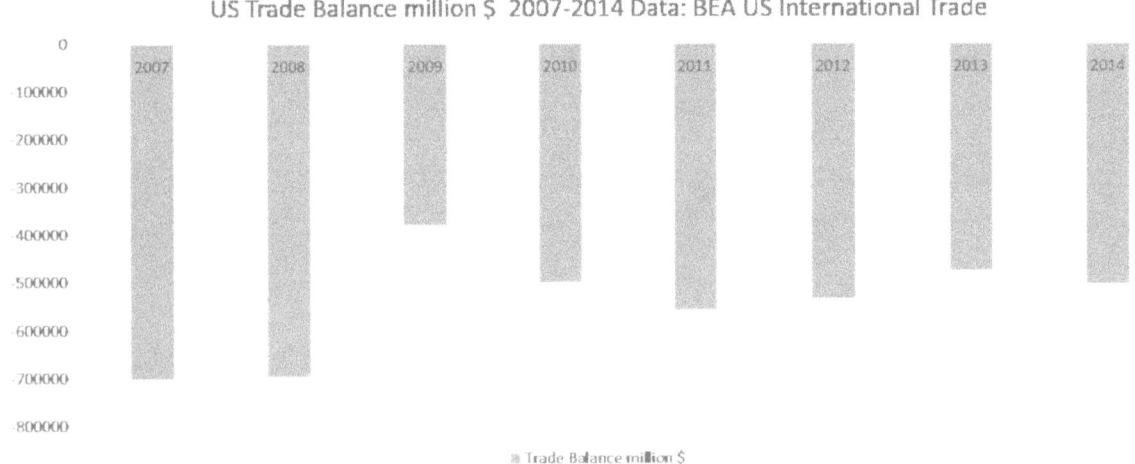

(Graph 18, Trade Balance. Data Source: BEA)

Trade balance shows balance between imports and exports. In other words, balance between spending and producing/earning/income.
Trade balance of the United States has been negative figures for a long time.
This means that the U.S. has been buying/spending/importing more than selling/earning/exporting.
This is really bad.

<Trade Balance with China>

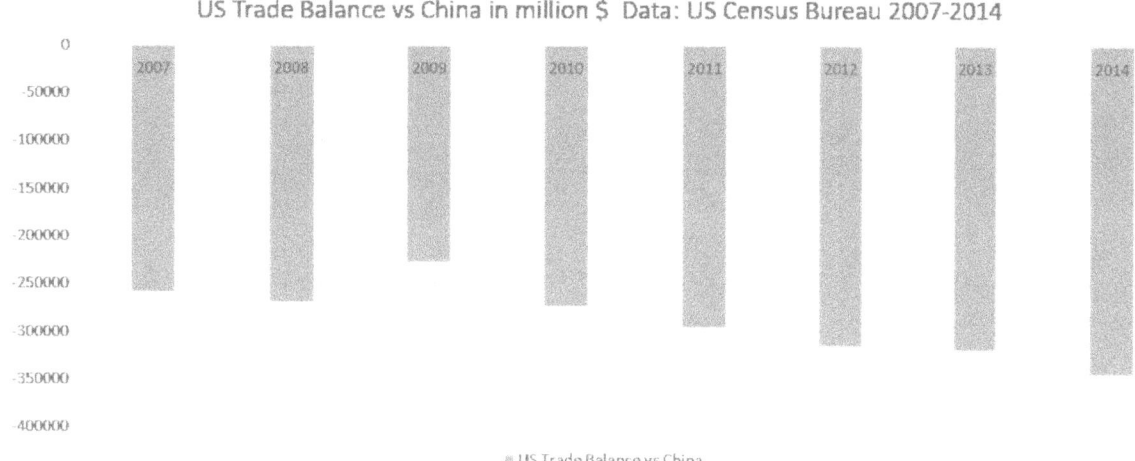

(Graph 19, Trade Balance with China. Data Source: US Census Bureau.)

<China's Contribution to the U.S. Trade Deficits in total.>

(Graph 20. The % of Trade deficits with China in total trade deficits.)

The trade balance with China has a majority of its share. The 68% of trade deficit comes from China in 2014.

<Trade Balance with China since 1985>

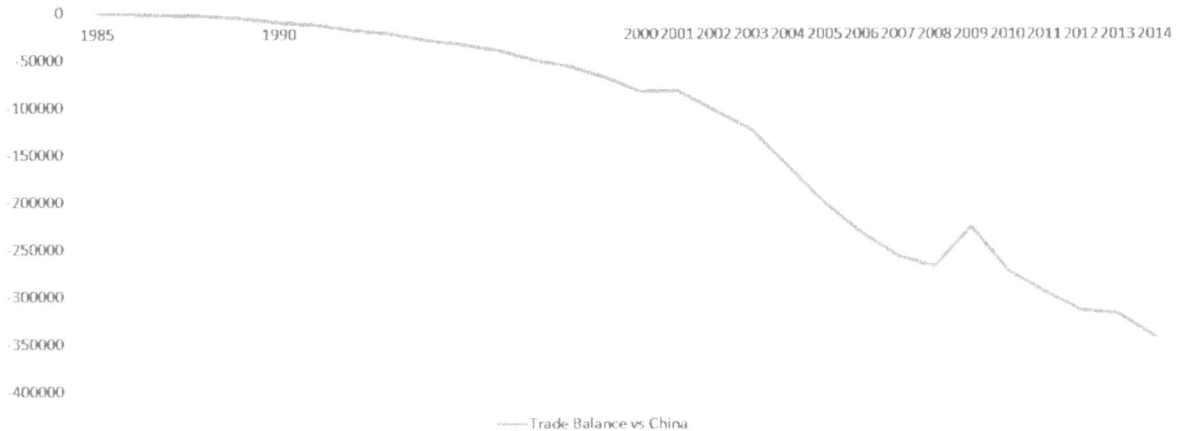

(Graph 21, Trade balance with China since 1985.)

The trade balance with China has been negative since 1985 and it is getting worse and worse since around year 2000.
This is really bad and threatening.

<Payment of the Trade deficit>

(Adam Smith's Era)
In Adam Smith's era, payment of the trade deficit was mainly done with gold and silver bullions.

(Now: Basically no actual payment and only accumulation of debts.)
In case of the United States, since paper money has basically no link with collateral securities such as gold and silver bullions, the debts are mainly financed by borrowing without collaterals, which means based on perceived trust or credibility only. IOU. If paper money, namely the U.S.$, were directly linked with gold and silver bullions, the United States must have had serious difficulties for clearing or paying back the debts a long time ago. Can you see that this is postponement of payments? Clever, isn't it?

However, this will become due in the end based on double ledger accounting method and nobody can escape from it including the U.S. except going on to defaults, which means bankruptcy.

1. Spend first. (Consumption driven economy)
2. Pay it on credit. (Financing by borrowing)(Selling the U.S. treasury bonds.)
3. Postponement of Payments => Accumulation of national debts.

What will happen in the end?

A disaster, right?

There is no such things as a free meal.

We have to pay for it in the end.

Do you know the earlier we pay, the easier the payment will be because of compound rate of interest?

In other words, we will suffer less if we act upon it now.

Why economists recommend it?

Because in economics theory, default is included.

Theory is basically the same as a game such as a trump game or a monopoly game.

What will happen when everybody goes bankrupt except one player in a monopoly game?

The game is over, right?

We play a new monopoly game from the scratch, right?

Here no pains are considered.

So is the economics theory.

In other words, economists will most likely recommend to go on defaults when it is absolutely necessary.

(For example.)

<"OK, this economics game is over. Let's play another economics game from the scratch.">

Do you know that the theory does not consider pains? The theory is just the same as a game. Ok, I lost or I failed, let's start a new game again from fresh. This is the same as going on defaults and start a new economics game again. In the real world, we will suffer lots of pains when the defaults happen. Lots of people will starve looking back to the history. People without enough savings will suffer most because another depression will last for years to recover. Based on my knowledge from reading a book, average American family has savings of about a couple of months, which is not enough for surviving for a couple of years during the next great depression when and only when it ever happens.

<Pain Factor is being ignored in economics theory.>

Economics theory is the same as an economics game on computer or a video game. Obviously pain factor is not considered or included. In video games, killing someone does not cause any pain because it is virtual. By the same token, going to default is not painful since it is in a world of pure mathematics.
1 + 1 = 2
2 − 1 = 1
This is not the same in the real world because a pain factor is included.

1 person + 1 person = 2 persons
2 persons − 1 person = 1 person.
Right?
No, it is not true in the real world.
Actually, "2 persons − 1 person = 1 person."
This means killing one person or elimination of one person, which will cause a severe pain or suffer.

By the same token, going on default will cause serious pains and suffers such as another great depression.
With respect to a pain factor, our economic activities are completely different from video games and thus economics theory. Therefore, going on default is not an option for us and thus it should be excluded from our choice or economic assumption in my opinion.

Historical debts of the Unites States are as follows:

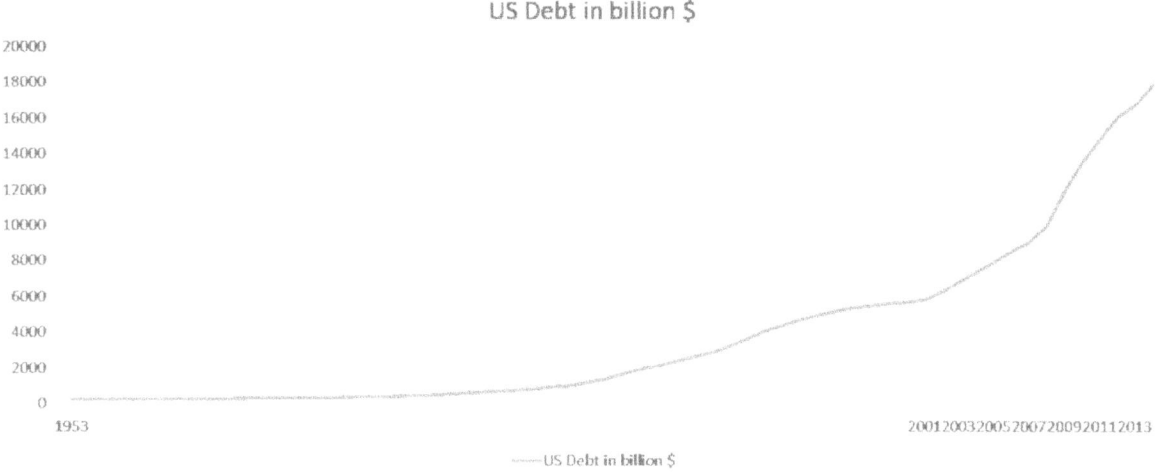

<The U.S. Historical Debts.>

(Graph 22, The U.S. historical debts. Data Source: Treasury Direct.)

The U.S. debts were very healthy before and around up to 1980.
I have a strong doubt that Nixon Shock in 1971 triggered expansion of the U.S. national debts because it declared cutting link between the U.S. $ and gold. In other words, the U.S. dollars have lost the anchor of gold.
The U.S. debt status has been getting really bad since around year 2000. Actually the U.S. debts were about tripled in about 14 years or so since year 2000. This is really bad considering compound rate of interest.
Unless we take corrective measures right now, it will be tripled again within 14 years or so. When this happen, most likely going for defaults will be the only option left.
In my opinion, the United States government is using inverse mechanism of capitalism as a nation. Everybody knows the theory of capitalism. Although the United States government definitely knows or acknowledges the theory, it is acting inversely to the theory or ignoring it. According to capitalism, capital produce gains, which is interest, and because of compound rate of interest, capital accumulation is the way to get rich. Inversely, the best way to become poor is the opposite. If the U.S. leave the trade deficits untreated as they are and finance them by borrowing, compound rate of interest will kill you in the end. Actually the trade deficit

is a loss of capital and interest payment is also another loss of capital with compound rate of interest, which will accelerate the loss. As Capital goes out, the country become less wealthy. This cycle is an inverse mechanism of capitalism. It is no wonder that the United States as a country is getting less affluent because of ever growing interest payments to the creditors including those who live outside of the United States.

In 2014, Interest payments are about 0.43 trillion $, which is a capital loss as opposed to a capital gain.

<GDP Growth>

GDP per capita $ with 1990 PPP conversion (source: Angus Maddison)

	1950	2001	
US	9,561	28,347	(About 3 X)
China	439	3,627	(About 8.3 X)
Japan	1,921	21,062	(About 10 X)
Germany	3,881	19,196	(About 5 X)
France	5,271	21,613	(About 4X)

(Without exchange rate adjustment)
(Data Source: Angus Maddison.)

GDP per capita growth of the U.S. is the smallest in the above.
GDP grew about 3 times in the past 50 years.
$(1 + 0.0225)^{50} = 3.042$
In other words, the U.S. GDP growth was about 2.25% in average in the past 50 years. This figure must be very close to inflation rate in my opinion. In other words, real GDP growth of the U.S. in the past 50 years will be close to zero considering inflation rate of roughly 2% or so if I am not mistaken! Almost no real growth or may be 1% growth in average or so! The above growth must be basically or largely nominal growth only considering inflation rate. In other words, the performance of the U.S. economy based on consumption driven for the past 50 years is quite disappointing based on the above data. Consumption driven economy is not working very well from economic growth point of view for the U.S. I got you in spite of your clever and beautiful economic tactics and veils.

<Huge gaps between expectations and actual results.>

> Although investors demand such as over 6 or 7 % of increase every year for publicly traded companies, actual performance of the U.S. as a whole was just about 2.25% increase for the past about 50 years in average. Obviously the system is not so working well.
> Investors are too demanding. Current business system is making the situation worse by firing managements and people too excessively. The real cause will not be the workers or managements but the business system itself. We need to change a definition or concept of the company as follows:
> From: Companies are for investors. (Now)
> To: Companies are not only for investors but also for the public. (From now on.)

<Hair and turtle race.>

<Interest rate is no problem>

> As Dr. Auerbach as well as economists say in economics theory that Interest rate will not go up when borrowing. Instead, interest rate of the U.S. treasury bills went down while money supply expansion through financing by borrowed money. Interest rate of the U.S. treasury bills were very low such as less than 2% or so in average after 2007/2008 financial crisis. This is also a sign of stagnant economy, though. When economy is good and prosperous, Production goes up, Employment goes up, Income goes up, and Interest rate must goes up because of increased demand for money/investment. Obviously, this kind of positive economic cycles have not been happening in the United States after the financial crisis if I am not mistaken.

<Interest Rate of Treasury Bonds in the U.S.>

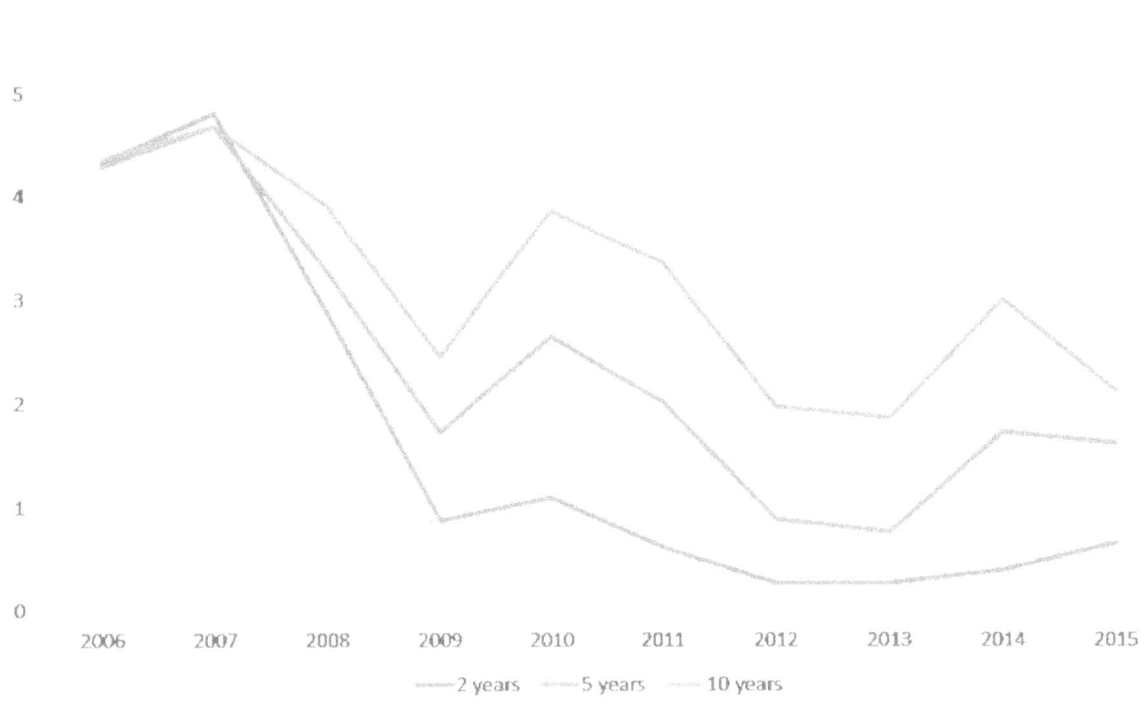

(Graph 23, interest rate when borrowing for the U.S. government. Data Source: treasury.gov.)

(Interest Rate when borrowing money for the U.S. government.)
This shows the interest rate when borrowing for the U.S. Government.
In other words, the U.S. government is paying very roughly about 2% of interest rate in average when borrowing between 2009 and 2015.

Note: The U.S. has national debts of about 18 trillion $ and interest payment alone amounts to about 0.43 trillion % these days.

The above only shows interest rate of US Treasury bonds just as an example. I am afraid that I have no comment on this because I actually do not know how US Treasury bonds are issued.
One thing I can say is that 2007/2008 incidents affected interest rate of US Treasury bonds very strongly by taking a look at the above graph. The Interest rate went down from 2007 to 2009 very sharply.

(No Actual Data collected when lending money for the U.S. government, sorry.)

I am afraid here that I did not collect actual interest rates for both borrowing and lending for the U.S. government/FRB. It is quite troublesome for me and also it will cost me some money for getting the data, sorry. Cheap money must mean almost zero interest or close to zero interest (roughly 0.00% - 0.25%) when money supply expansion happened which I do not pretend to know. (Target range of federal fund rate was around 0.00%-0.25% between 2009 and 2015.)

(My Explanations)

If I am not mistaken, the following are my explanations:
- Banks make profits from the difference between lending and borrowing money.
- When FRB expanded money supply during 2007/2008 and afterwards, federal fund rate of interest went down to almost zero. (Cheap money) (Target rage: around 0.00%-0.25% between 2009 and 2015) In other words, the U.S. banks could borrow money at almost no cost from FRB. This is the rate of lending money for the U.S. government/FRB, which is federal fund rate.
- The U.S. banks of course try hard to lend money at the highest rate in the market but in the end the U.S. banks can also buy the U.S. Treasury bonds (Lending money to the U.S. government) as long as it is justifiable, which means interest rates of treasury bonds are higher than inflation rate. The U.S. banks can keep holding the U.S. Treasury bonds when they could not sell them to their customers.

(Lending rate of interest for the U.S. banks.)

Prime rate = When the U.S. banks lend money to companies.
Prime rate = approximately federal fund rate +3%.
In other words, when federal fund rate is 0.25%, prime rate will be about 3.25%, although I do not pretend to know the real deals.

When federal fund rate goes down, the U.S. banks can lend money cheaper to companies.

Basically speaking, the U.S. banks can make gross margin of about 3%, which is the difference between borrowing and lending rate, the difference between federal fund rate and prime rate.

- As far as I checked, inflation rate (CPI) at 2007/2008 was 4% at the highest and mostly less than 4%. This might be one of the reasons why the interest rates of the US Treasury bonds were pulled down to very low level especially in 2009 based on my observations.

As long as banks are motivated to buy the U.S. Treasury bonds, it creates demand and thus FRB can supply money to them proportionately without increasing its interest rates as an explanation.

For complete analysis or explanations, please ask for it to economists those who are experts on this matter.

In addition, theoretically speaking and also according to Dr. Auerbach, interest rate will not go up when the government finance it by borrowing. When printing money, it causes inflation, though.

<Measure of Inflation>

We can check inflation trends by looking at WPI and CPI.

<WPI, wholesale price index>

Although this is yearly data, it looks fine. I do not see any unhealthy inflation trend at all.

<WPI since 1960 in the U.S.>

(Graph 24, WPI since 1960. Data Source: indexmundi.com)

WPI shows inflation rate at whole sale level. When we do business, companies buy goods at wholesale price and thus this shows inflation rate of industry/business level or deals.

The above graph shows that whole sale price index got almost doubled in the past 55 years or so, which is healthy as far as I know.

$(1+r)^{55} = 2$

$(1+0.012)^{55} = 1.927$

Very roughly speaking, average growth rate of WPI in the past about 55 years is about 1.2%, which is actually very low. In other words, inflation rate at wholesale level is about 1.2% in average in the past about 55 years.
We can see some impact of 2007/2008 incidence as a spike in the above.

<WPI, 2006-2014 in the U.S.>

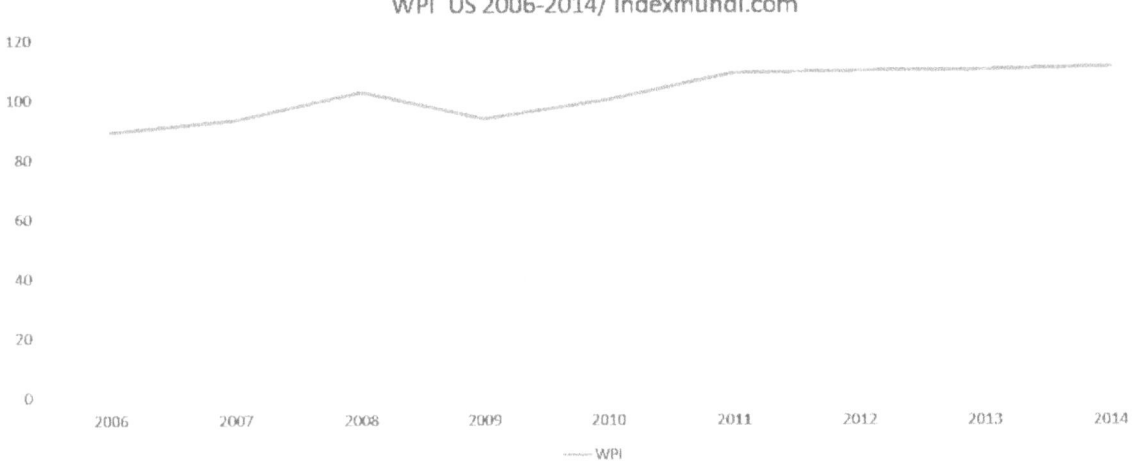

(Graph 25, WPI 2006-2014. Data Source: indexmundi.com)

As you can see, WPI went down in 2009, which is a sign of deflation.

<CPI, consumer price index in the U.S.>

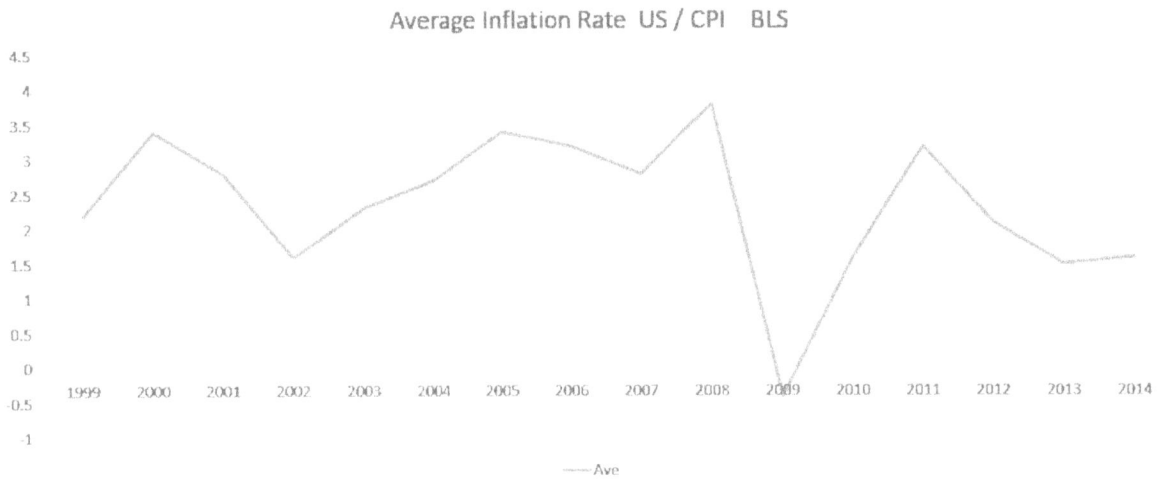

(Graph 26, CPI. Data Source: Bureau of labor statistics.)

Note: We can clearly see an impact of 2007/2008 incidence in the above. CPI went to a negative figure in 2009, which is deflation. The U.S. economy must have been in danger in 2009 based on the above graph.

Except 2009, inflation rate was around between 1.5% and 4% between 1999 and 2014.

<CPI in the U.S.>

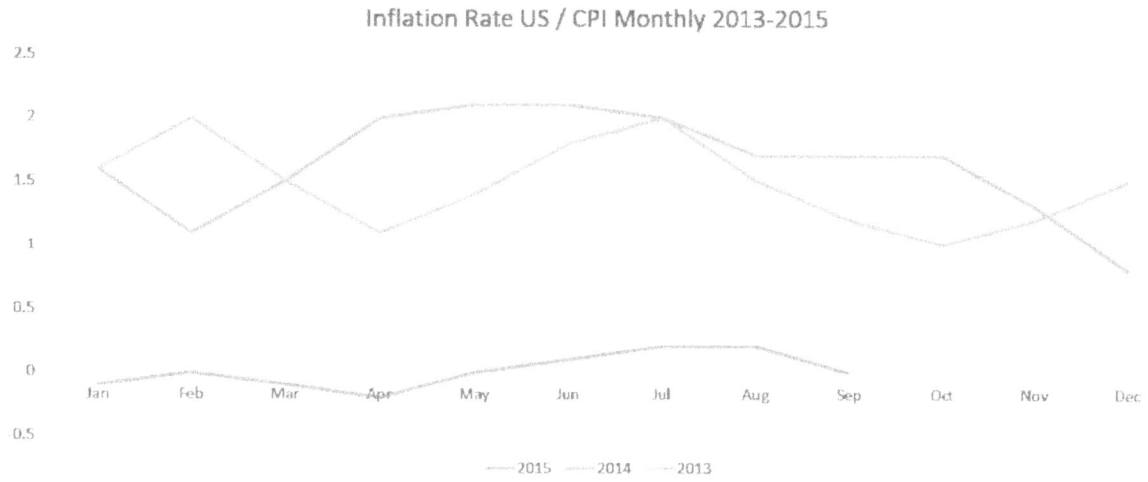

(Graph 27, CPI 2013-2015. Data Source: Bureau of labor statistics.)

The above is monthly data of CPI between 2013 and 2015.
CPI shows inflation rate of consumer price or at retail.
When we talk about inflation rate, we usually talk about this rate.
Inflation rate stayed between 1% and 2 % range between 2013 and 2014.
Since the beginning of 2015, it seems like showing some sign of deflation because CPI staggering around at zero range for the past nine months or so in 2015.

CPI 2015
Jan   -0.1
Feb   0.0
Mar   -0.1
Apr   -0.2
May   0.0
Jun   0.1
Jul   0.2

Aug   0.2
Sep   0.0

Considering growth business model and pro-inflation model of current economic theory, the economy looks a little stagnant according to CPI figures in 2015.
Other than that, it seems to be no problem.

<Median Household Income in the U.S.>

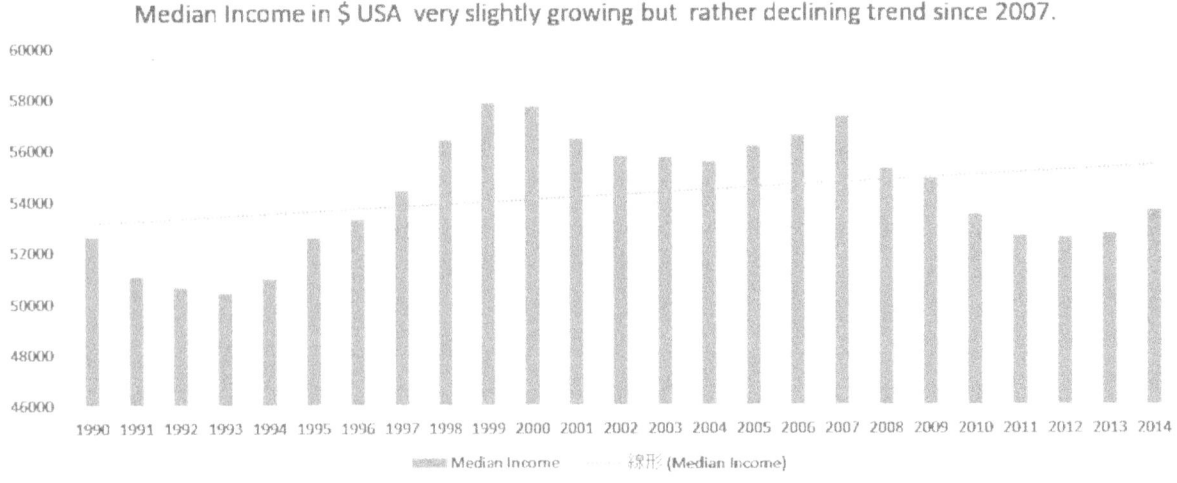

(Graph 28, median house hold income. Data Source: statista.com)

The above graph basically shows a trend of median income household in the United States. It looks bad in my opinion.

It seems that income of middle class is not growing very much. Instead, it is declining from 2007 to 2013. In 2014, it went up a little bid, though.

Year   (m $)
2007   57.3
2008   55.3
2009   54.9

2010 53.5
2011 52.7
2012 52.6
2013 52.8
2014 53.7
(Data Source: statista.com)
(I rounded up figures in order to avoid infringement. Please just see the trend only.)

This trend is not consistent with or contradictory to Dow Jones's strong increasing trend.

This can be partly explained by outsourcing and off-shore manufacturing tendency of the big U.S. companies such as listed at Dow Jones. In other words, when Consumption went up, Supply went up. If this were only done by domestic production, Employment would go up and Income would go up accordingly.

However, since lots of production were done at foreign countries such as in China, Employment and Income went up at a manufacturing-hub such as in China. I do not see much income growth of median income household in the United States. When Production (in China) went up, Income in the U.S. did not go up very much because of not many productions in the U.S. anymore. Instead, Income in China must have gone up because of its manufacturing-hub function for the U.S.

In other words, in economics theory of a confined market or in a single country market, there must be a very strong correlation between Dow Jones' trend and Median Income of the U.S. household's trend. It seems to be no correlation between the two based on my rough data observations of the above graph without running correlation analysis. It could be found out when we run correlation analysis which I do not have any access for it right now, I am sorry.

It seems that the U.S. companies are doing well based on Dow Jones but they left American labor forces behind in the United States with respect to Production/Employment. Most factories are located in oversees such as in Chia, for example. It means that this whole system is making American workers idle by taking factory jobs away from them. A cycle of spending money and making money is not functioning properly here. It never will. The same system, the same result. In other words, laissez faire or free economy is not good enough to function satisfactory under the current global conditions. We need to adjust it manually unfortunately. Therefore, I am recommending conditional free economy with minimum regulations. We have the same situations in Japan, though.

We called it a vacuum effect or doughnut phenomena in Japan.

We have lost lots of factory jobs in Japan, too. We have lost lots of employment accordingly as a result.

Who is bad? Nobody is bad.

I blame it on our whole system such as cruel, over-demanding, and job-threatening business system as well as unfit economic system for the changed environments/conditions. We need to change our business system by changing a concept of the company such as follows:

Now (From): Company is for investors.
New (To): Company is not only for investors but also for the public.

Investors can demand on the condition that it does not hurt the public interest. In other words, we should control investors' becoming too demanding. This is similar to a salary cap for professional sports.

<Apply the theory on the earth basis.>

First of all, applying single country based economic models on current global economy, which are based on multi-countries situation, is not appropriate or unfit. This is the violation of Use Instructions.

If we do want to apply current economic models, we need to apply it on the earth basis, which is a confined market. For this purpose, we need an earth government to implement it.

<Free Economy>

Engagement with China itself is a violation of free economy.
The followings are my logics:

1. Integer plus integer equals integer.
   Integer + Integer = Integer.
2. Integer + non-integer = Non-integer.
   By the same token,
   Free economy + Free economy = Free economy.
   Free economy + Non-free economy = Non-free economy.

Where the United States = Free economy, but China =Non-free economy or controlled economy.

Therefore, the U.S. economy + Chinese economy = Non-free economy or partially manipulated economy by China.

Since Chia's economic impact was getting larger and larger because of her growing economic presence such as the second biggest GDP in the world now.

The United States is applying free economy theory on non-free economy situation right now considering her engagement with China. This is why theory of free economy does not work as intended or as the theory promises. Basic assumptions of laissez-faire is violated since China is controlling economy for her own advantage right now. Nobody controls or manipulates his/her economy for the other's benefit. If somebody wants to control his/her economy, it must be always of his/her own benefits.

Given that current economy is non-free, we should use economic models for non-free economy such as conditional free economy, for instance.

Conditional free economy means that intervention of free economy on the condition when it hurts the public interests. The public interest means that of the whole earth instead of a single country. This includes when the economy is not working properly/well or free-economy becomes inappropriate such as emergency or semi-emergency situations.

Chapter 5: Going back to basics.

<Going back to basics>

Production = Consumption.

What we produce, we can consume.
Basically this is a rule in life or in nature.
When hunter gatherer era, what we hunted and gathered, we could consumed.

<Natural cycle>

Production first and consumption afterwards.
Production (+) = Consumption (-)
Work (+) = Spending (-)/Reward
There is a cycle of production and consumption here.

<Reversed cycle and delayed payment by economists.>

(Consumption only and no actual payment so far.)

(This is a trick being conducted by economists)

Economists reversed the natural cycle as follows:
Consumption first and postpone payment as late as possible.
Consumption = Principal x (1+ interest rate)^x
Reward/consumption first = Work afterwards + pains (interest payments)

Now our story is reversed and 180 degrees opposite based on recommendation of current economists, so to speak, Consumption driven economy.
This created a vicious cycle in terms of payments as follows:
Overconsumption + debts for the past 60 years or so.
We are encouraged to spend and consume as much as possible to facilitate economy. What happened in the end? We created huge national debts such as 18 trillion dollars in the United States.

Please do not blame on economists due to the following reasons:
No body became an over-spender or consumption maniac without his or her consent! It is our fault if we became over-spenders even though novel laurate economists recommend it.

My explanations are as follows:

1. Production minas (-) Consumption = Savings (+) or debts (-).
   In nature, Production (P) = Consumption (C).
   $P = C$
   This is also true for barter trade.
2. Trade Balance = Exports minas (-) Imports.
   Exports = Surplus produce.
   Imports = shortage of produce. (Consumption)
   In the United States, Trade balance has been consecutively negative since 1976 or even earlier.
   Exports < Imports
   Surplus produce < Shortage of produce (Consumption)

   (Consumption > Production)
   In other words, consumptions are bigger than productions as a whole in the U.S. consecutively for the past 40 years or more.
   People in the US are spending more than producing. This will not last forever, though.
   Why is that?
   It is because novel laurate economists recommends consumption-driven economy. This is an authority effect. If novel laurate economists are saying, something must be in it beyond my comprehension, which is what I thought first. As far as I have found out so far, nothing was in it. Economists just reversed the order of the natural cycle.
   We cannot afford consumption-driven economy anymore.
   Unfortunately we have to make our ends meet considering $18 trillion of national debts.
   We need to consume less and produce more.

We need to be more productive. We need to increase productive labor. We need to reduce unproductive labor.

We need to take less holidays and days off instead of increasing those in order to produce more.

In other words, Industry driven economy should be our choice in the future. Produce first and consume afterwards. This is consistent with the cycle of nature but most likely you do not like it. We can spend more when using consumption driven economy as long as we can pay for it. We can no longer afford it considering amounts of about 18 trillion $ of national debts and thus we have to abandon it and change it.

Industry driven economy will be most logical and a sure way for rebuilding our business and economy from now on.

Chapter 6. Adam Smith's Teachings.

(Adam Smith: Pro parsimony.)

Do you know Adam Smith never recommended consumption driven economy?

Adam Smith says as follows:

"Capitals are increased by parsimony, and diminished by prodigality and misconduct." (Chapter III, Book II, "the Wealth of Nations".)

"…every prodigal appears to be a public enemy, and every frugal man a public benefactor." (Chapter III, Book II, "the Wealth of Nations".)

"….As the capital of an individual can be increased only by he saves from his annual revenue or his annual gains, so the capital of a society, which is the same with that of all the individuals who compose it, can be increased only in the same manner."
(Chapter III, Book II, "the Wealth of Nations".)

In short, Adam Smith says as follows:
(Adam Smith's wisdom)

- Frugal + saving = Capital increase.
- The above is also true for a society.

- Prodigality and misconduct => Capital Diminution.

Prodigal means over-spending, right?

What will happen, overspending + increased holidays?
Increased national debts, right?

This is exactly what is happening in the U.S.
The system is wrong. Consumption driven economy is wrong in terms of accumulation of wealth or capitals.

Actually Adam Smith is against consumption driven economy based on the above stated sentences!

The U.S. lost lots of capitals by way of increasing national debts because of prodigality and misconduct.
The U.S. increased unproductive labor by increasing holidays which must be regarded as misconduct in the above sentences.
 Who is right, Adam Smith or novel laurate economists?
Adam Smith is right based on the data we have in every respects.

Also Adam Smith repeatedly emphasized importance of frugality and paying attention to a trade balance in his book. He also mentioned that war is very expensive and war expenses placed heavy burdens on the British economy in his era.

<War Expense>

The United States started creating debts since 1953 or earlier.
I didn't collect the data before 1950, I am afraid.

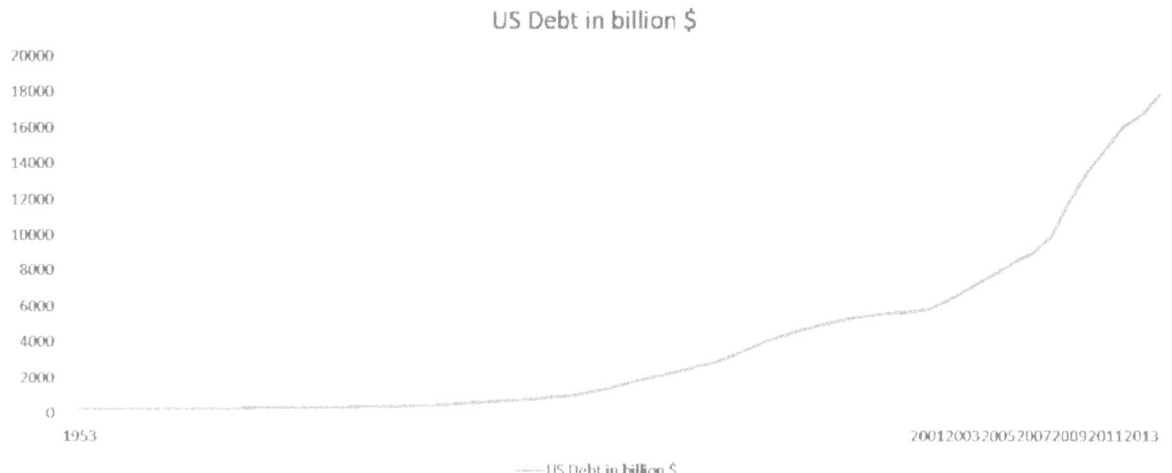

(Graph 29, the U.S. national debts.)

Note: The national debts became almost 65 times as much comparing 1953 and 2014.
1953: 275 billion $
2014: 17,824 billion $

<Korean War>

Korean War was between 1950 and 1953.
It says that in 1953, South Korea and the United States concluded a Mutual Defense Treaty.
This cannot be just a coincidence.
The above mentioned mutual Defense Treaty must have something to do with the U.S. National debts based on my observation and wild hunch.
Wars are expensive. The U.S. went on Vietnam War, Cold War, etc.

<GDP>

GDP = (Gross Domestic) Product
Production = P
Labor = productive labor + unproductive labor
Labor = L
Productive labor = p_1
Unproductive labor = p_0
L = $p_1 + p_0$
P = f (Labor, resources, capitals, and technologies)
Holidays are unproductive.
Although I have never read the bible, the bible says that work 6 days a week and take one day off.
How many holidays do you have in the United States right now?
$P_1 = L - p_0$
The more holidays you take, the less productive working days are available or left.
Dr. Auerbach once said in his class that "people work less when a country gets rich". This is happening in the United States right now.
In the United States, the national debts were about tripled in the past 15 years and amounts to about 18 trillion dollars now.
This is an emergency situation. Why?
It will be tripled again for the coming 15 years or so unless the United States changes its system or apply economics theory differently.
The same system, the same result.

The same process, the same result.
What is wrong?
1. Consumption driven economy.
2. Increasing unproductive labor.
   Making the country less productive.
   By increasing holidays (unproductive labor) and thus decreasing productive labor in the United States in my opinion.
   Nothing is wrong with consumption-driven economy as long as we can afford it. We can no longer afford consumption driven economy in my opinion considering the amounts of the national debts in the U.S.

<Cycles>

Ups and downs.
Good and bad.
Pros and cons.
Work and reward.
Production and consumption.
Borrowing and paying.
In other words, this is a swing of pendulum.

<Only pleasure and reward will not last forever. >

In the U.S., we have surplus consumption for more than the past 60 years or so.
Logically speaking, the country will go bankrupt in the end unless she stops her bleeding or stops overconsumption and start paying off her debts.

<Usual cycle>

Usual cycle is as follows:
Work/production and (=) consumption.
Surplus produce (export) and (=) surplus consumption (import).

<In case of the U.S.>

Surplus consumption, surplus consumption, surplus consumption, forever.
Debts, debts, and debts, for the past 60 years or so.
Nobody and no country can afford it forever.

It is a question of a chicken first or an egg first.
In the past or in nature, production first and consumption next or afterwards.
Right now, consumption first and production next or payment later as long as you can pay for it in the U.S.
What will happen if the United States goes on default?
It will create a disaster such as another great depression, by which everybody will suffer including you and me in my opinion. Lots of us will lose our jobs by looking back at the history of the Great Depression in 1929.
This is why I am giving a caution right now.
Which is better either reactive or proactive?
Proactive is better than reactive, right?
Here I am talking about taking a proactive action.
It is time to change our spending habits and couch potatoes habits in addition to obtaining saving habits. In other words, we need to change everything including our habits, life styles, our business system, and our economic system altogether. Since all of these are related and inter-connected, we will never be successful by changing just only one or two. We can only be successful when we change them all together at once "gradually".
Industry driven economy should be a way to go.
This is a mundane solution and thus I tend to believe that not many people will buy my proposal.
This is not as fancy or attractive as consumption driven economy.
However, consumption driven economy is similar to a short term gain and a long term pain scenario.
Yes, we enjoyed consumption/spending first which will not last forever because this is done by just postponement of payments.
In the end, we have to pay for it. Otherwise, we will disgrace our ancestors such as Benjamin Franklin.
We can quit or finish playing this economic game and start a totally new economic game all over again, which is going for default.

If we decide to do this, lots of people will definitely lose our jobs, etc. because of inevitably causing another great depression, which will last for years. If we do not have enough savings, we might go to starve.

<Frugal>

I did not invent it. Many successful people and many affluent people are frugal in the U.S. Yes, some of them are not frugal but they are short lived. In the long run those people spent up most of their money and would become poor again. Successful people work hard and long hours, and save some money in their life time based on numbers of books including "The Millionaire Next Door."

This book says that over two million copies sold. At least 2 million people or so must know about how to get rich by frugality, hardworking habit, and saving habit.

Do you know that these are not good enough to be successful or rich as a country for the following two reasons?
1. In democracy, only a majority of opinion counts.
2. Only action counts. Knowledge alone will not make you rich.

1. In the United States as a country, there are about 320 million people. 2 million people represents less than 1% of the population. This is also consistent with the data I have. Less than 1% of population is very rich in the United States.

   Anyway, over 160 million people or a majority of the U.S. population need to acknowledge that the way to become rich as a nation is that a majority of people should be frugal, hardworking, and saving money. A country is just an aggregate of individuals or its inhabitants/members. A country is the same as a team of inhabitants. When lots of people are over-spenders and idle, the country will become less affluent and less competitive in the long run. The country is just a reflection of each of us as a group.

2. Only actions count. I know that people in the U.S. have the highest education in the world and you have more than sufficient knowledges to

be rich and successful and indeed the U.S. has been the most successful country so far. However, it is not good enough to become affluent as a nation by taking a look at amounts of the national debts, which are the results of your past performance as a whole or as a nation. Here, I am not talking about individual performance per se at all. Even though a majority of people know how to get rich, they still need to act upon it. Only action counts instead of just having knowledges. For example, if lots of people are taking many holidays and work less and less hours by increasing unproductive labor, it really does not matter how smart you are and how knowledgeable you are. Labor = Productive labor (1) + unproductive labor (0).

$P1 = L - P0$

When you increase unproductive labor, you will inevitably decrease productive labor proportionately.

In other words, only productive labor (P1) counts. If you increase the quantity of unproductive labor (P0) while keeping the quantity of Labor constant, you will get less P1(less productive labor). (=Produce less)
If you produce less and spend/consume more, you will create a national debt in the end, right?
This is what current economists are suggesting and leading us to end up huge national debts.

I do not need to be an economic PH.D to figure it out.

This is very simple. I only used addition and subtraction here.

<Authority Effect of Current Economists.>

In psychology it is called an authority effect. When an authority said a certain thing, people tend to blindly believe/accept it without questioning about it, which is a blind obedience.
By the way, only some economists proposed consumption-driven economy, which is current main stream economists in the United States, I guess.

<Forgetting about Adam Smith's teachings.>

Adam Smith never said that. Adam Smith emphasized frugality which is 180 degree opposite to consumption-driven economy.
Which is correct?

Looking at the amounts of national debts in the United States, Adam Smith must be right.
Do you know that consumption driven economy is almost identical to the way I treat my dog?
I give lots of food to my dog because she looks happy when she ate full. When my dog gets hungry she irritates me a lot for requesting more foods. I am a human being and thus better than just an animal or dog. I do not have to consume more and more. Do not treat me like my dog or an animal, which is what I feel about consumption driven economy.
Do you know that this is also something to do with our current business system of ever growing nature?
Since the business system is cruel, people get tortured or threaten to be fired in business or at work, smart people must have figured out how to tame or pacify people at off-work situation. One way must be a consumption driven economy which induces dopamine or works as an opiate.
This is one way of making people addictive to consumption and thus make us more controllable or manageable in my opinion.

In summary, our current whole systems are inappropriate or unfit for the current conditions and thus when we need to change them. We can no longer afford to use consumption driven economy.

Current system is inappropriate because of the followings:
Current system is ever growing system and when we stop growing, penalties are waiting for us such as getting fired when we missed the budget/target, which is most likely around 6% of growth every year, which is exponential.
  $(1.06)^T$ where T = time or year.
  $(1.06)^{10} = 1.79$
In other words, in 10 years we have to grow as much as 80% under the expectation of our current business system.
  This is an infinite model, by the way.

On the other hand, the earth is geographically limited or finite and also resources are clearly getting short these days. We are clearly seeing physical limitations right now.

We are living in a finite environment here.

It is illogical to apply an infinite model on a finite situation.

This is one of the reasons why we have so many cheating or manipulations such as accounting scandals, etc. these days.

Actually, GDP growth of the U.S. for the past 50 years or so is just 2.25% in average including inflation rate. While growth requirement for companies is around 6%, actual performance as a country is just 2.25% in average. Don't you think that the target is too high or investors are too demanding? It is no wonder that people get fired very often in business world.

When our job security is being threatened, people act illogically and also try to save our jobs no matter what.

When we are forced to do or achieve impossible things, it is our animal nature that induce cheating. We start protecting our jobs, families, lives, and subsistence. We need to buy milk to feed our baby no matter what.

This is preservation of species, which is intrinsically embedded
In our animal brain.

Then what should we do?

We should change our system from an infinite model to a finite model accordingly.

We should stop using the growth model.

<Circular Economy>

Our end goal should be CIRCULAR ECONOMY of Ms. Ellen MacArthur in my opinion.

CIRCULAR ECONOMY is not a growth model according to my understanding. Its assumption is a pond situation or people on the boat situation where we have no room for growth and thus we have to recycle everything. Under this conditions we can only afford a certain number of population. Growth of population beyond a certain level will not be suitable for our survival.

By the way, according to information of Mr. Richard Bensons' book, affordable population on the earth is about 5 billion based on calculations by scientists. We have 7.3 billion population now and thus we are supposed to reduce consumption as much as 30%. 7.3 x 0.7= 5.11

Do you agree with me that we can no longer afford consumption driven economy anymore?

CIRCULAR ECONOMY is basically status quo or no growth, which is like marching on the same spot without moving forward.

On the other hands, our current system is marching forward for ever or even running forward as fast as possible.

We have to slow down before stalling.

How could we slow down our current economy of marching forward very fast?

<Conditional Free Economy>

My proposal here is conditional free economy with minimum intervention or regulations.

Free economy on the condition that it does not hurt the public interests (of the earth.)

Conditional means laws, regulations, and restrictions imposed by the EARTH GOVERNMENT, which we do not have yet.

Chapter 7. Monopoly.

<Monopolies are not acceptable.>

(We definitely have to do something about unmanaged monopolies right now.)

Note: I use monopolies for the meaning of a monopoly, duopoly, and oligopoly, all of which are unhealthy conditions.

Right now earth companies are acting freely without being controlled by anti-monopoly laws, for example, and thus conditions are kind of out of control or chaotic.

Somebody needs to initiate creating the EARTH GOVERNMENT project please because I am not qualified for it.

Do you know that taxing will slow down economy? According to Adam Smith, it is. This is one of the reason why the U.S. economists are reluctant to propose Tax increase.

If we want to slow down economy somewhat, we can increase tax on luxuries, for example, though.

Chapter 8. Deregulations.

<Deregulations>

This is "a short term gain and a long term pain."

Deregulation will create a room for expansion and new competition and thus it is good when the market get stagnant such as in a monopolistic situation.

However, it is a matter of time that the market will become stagnant again under the current economic system because it will create another new monopolies, which are bigger this time.

This time, our situation will get worse because we now have bigger companies of fewer numbers which leaves us bigger monopolies and it will become harder to solve.

In micro economics class, Dr. Mark Johnson showed/taught us a monopoly model. It is all mathematical formulas and it proves that in free market as time goes by, it will create a monopoly in the end. In other words, if we leave companies under free competition, it will inevitably create a monopoly condition in the end, which is mathematically proved and this is happening right now in the real world.

This is called constructive destructions according to Mr. Munger.

In my opinion, this is nothing but the last man standing economics game. This is one of the reasons that companies are getting bigger and bigger these days. Actually many companies are so huge that even American Government can no longer control them according to Mr. Al Gore's book.

I have no comment on that because I am not recommending free economy from now on.

Yes, free economy must be the best under the curtain range or healthy conditions. What I am saying is that our current conditions are getting off range or not healthy anymore. Therefore, free economy will not be the best choice under the current conditions of unhealthy and semi-emergency. Under the conditional free economy, such kind of huge companies will be restricted by anti-monopoly laws and regulations enforced by the EARTH GOVERNMET.

Right now anti-monopoly regulations are not working properly or forceful enough to control or prevent monopolies.

In other words, we have to handle and control monopolies properly. Failure of controlling monopolies is one of the reasons of economic malfunctioning these days.

We are unable to control/handle monopolies without having an earth government right now.

Chapter 9 TPP.

<TPP>

This is also "a short term gain and a long term pain," which is basically the same as deregulations.

TPP will create opportunities of geographical expansion by providing a bigger market.

Therefore, firstly it is good for member countries, although some of member countries will become losers and only winner countries will gain. Basically this is the same as deregulations with respect to the aftereffects of creating bigger monopolies.

Secondly, it is bad for non-member countries because TPP will work as a kind of block economy against non-member countries. If my understanding is correct, block economy is one of the trigger for the WWII. Economically weak countries will suffer most such as countries in Africa, etc.

I worry about left over countries without belonging to any economic community such as African countries. I assume that stand alone small independent countries will not survive as they are unless those countries become a member of one of economic blocks/communities such as EU and TPP in my opinion.

In the end, this situation will become economically unstable and dangerous and thus we should become one as a whole ASAP, which means establishing a new EARTH GOVERNMENT.

Chapter 10. Symptoms V.S. A Real Cause.

<Symptoms V.S. A Real Cause>
We need to treat real causes instead of just treating symptoms.

(Symptoms)   (A Real Cause)
Cheating   Cruel ever-growing and unfit business model
Mal-practices in business

Solution, for example.
Change the current business system, which is the real cause.

(Now)   (Future)
Companies are for investors. Companies are not only for investors but also for the public (the Earth)

Chapter 11. A New Business Model.
<Conditionally Free Business Model>

A Definition or Concept:
Publicly traded companies should be not only for investors but also for the public.

In other words, companies are free to pursue their own interests on the condition that they do not hurt the public interests.
Public interests in this case include our survival needs such as preservations of natural resources, for example.
To be more specific, we do not want any companies grow too fast and pursue ever looking for growth and improvement at maximum speed.
Abandon consumption driven economy.
Instead, we want to slow down our economic activities gradually for the sake of our survival needs.
Actually we cannot afford much competition when emergency or semi-emergency conditions we will be facing.
Under this kind of conditions, we have to work together corroborate each other instead of competing.

<Two Systems go hand on hand>
1. Consumption driven economy.
2. Current Business System.

Consumption driven economy is a pacifier in my opinion.
Unless we are being tortured by cruel, ever growing, and unfit business system at work, we do not need to be pacified from the beginning.
Therefore, some clever people, most likely novel laurate economists, have proposed consumption driven economy in the past when conditions are different from now, I guess.
First of all, since consumption driven economy is unfit now and self-killing considering our survival needs, we should give it up.
However, we are currently being tortured at our work because of unfit business system also.

Unless both the unfit business model and the unfit economic system are changed together simultaneously, the change will never work or be successful.

In other words, both consumption driven economy and cruel ever growing business system need to be abandoned altogether simultaneously.

Using both industry driven economy and conditionally free business model is recommended.

<Our Future>

Nobody can predict our future and thus this is just my biased projections for our future.

1. CIRCULAR ECONOMY:

    We will be destined to use the CIRCULAR ECONOMY proposed by Ms. Ellen MacArthur in the end. In this situation, we will be living like a monk eating healthy diet such as lots of grains and vegetables with occasional supplements of fish and meats, for example. Everything will be recycled. We gain our satisfactions from our daily meditations, chanting, or arts, music, dancing, etc.

    I noticed that this is very similar to lives of Amish People in the U.S. Main difference may be that Amish people do not use electricity while we can still use electricity derived from solar and wind power, I guess. I am very sure that we can live like this although current life styles are more enjoyable and preferable as far as we can afford it.

    Actually in Japan at Edo era, about 1600 to 1900 AD, we lived isolated from the rest of the world. Japan closed its door and people lived pretty much confined in Japan, which is similar to CIRCULAR ECONOMY according to my understanding.

    It is not so bad. In this condition, people have to live together in harmony. Downside will be that competition will be less and thus advancement will be very slow or static. We will face a new danger or threat from outsiders such as aliens from outer space, though.

    In this era, Japan has developed its original culture such as GABUKI (similar to musicals), HAIKU (poems), UKIOE (painting arts), etc.

    People are subject to be changed when the environment changes.

We have to adjust to our changed environments. Otherwise, we will go extinct.
When our resources get scarce, we consume/spend less and eat less accordingly. We cannot afford consumption driven economy anymore.
Which is first, a chicken or an egg?
It really does not matter which is first because in the end we have to change whether voluntarily or involuntarily.

A necessity is a mother of invention.
We can change our habits, life styles, and our behaviors although it requires some disciplines.

Chapter 12. Conditional Free Economy and Conditional Democracy.
<Conditional free economy and conditional democracy>

On the condition that it does not hurt the public interests.

Actually this is a contingency plan and an emergency execution when the public interest gets hurt.

Here I am talking about the situation right now. As economy grows, population will grow inevitably because of increased subsistence. As the population grow, natural resources will be more getting scarce and also the Climate Change will be accelerated. Logically speaking, we should manage both population growth and economic growth for the sake of our survival, which are unmanaged right now.

I derive this from Human Body mechanism or analogy. Under normal situation, human brain is in control. In other words, we act logically and make logical decisions. However, when emergency situation or we get panic, animal brain takes it over due to survival need or preservation of species instinct. In this abnormal situation, people act illogically and make illogical decisions.

The same thing or mechanism must apply to our current economy, which is based on human behaviors.

Economics theory only works under the certain conditions which is healthy and normal conditions.

The current economics theory is unfit and not working properly or well right now because our current situation is no longer healthy nor normal.

One of the reasons is the violation of assumptions as follows:

(Logical thinking and logical behavior when healthy conditions only.)
  - Assumption of logical thinking and logical behaviors.

People are not machines. People's mind and action are subject to be changed according to the situations.

In other words, the current economics theory will not work properly when people get panic since people will not act logically.

Panic persons will often times act illogically in order to save their jobs, subsistence, or securities at the expense of the public interests. This is why I am recommending conditional free economy when conditions get worse and people start acting illogically.

Expansion model is unfit under limited or scarce resources situations right now.

Theory of free economy is for a single country. It is a model for a confined market. Unless we can secure these basic assumptions of a confined market, the current economics theory will not work well as it is intended.

For example, there are two types of camel, one has only one hump and the other has two humps.

Economists created a perfect saddle for one hump camel and they boost of how perfect it is as long as basic assumptions are met, which is the case with one hump camel.

Suppose here we have a camel of two humps and economists say that this saddle is perfect and insist to use it for the camel with two humps. It is obvious that this is unfit and will not work well.

However, the economists or authorities say that this theory should work because the theory is perfect. Because of an authority effect, laypersons blindly follow experts' opinion, which is a majority of population. In the end, after following experts' opinion, we ended up creating huge national debts by financing by borrowing while ignoring fundamental principle of Capitalism, which is the compound rate of interest, for example.

Here I am talking about misapplication of economics theory. Although the theory itself is perfect, we are applying it on inadequate conditions and environments. The current economics theory is fundamentally unfit for the current environments, where there exist multiple countries economically interwoven each other such as a global market right now.

Why? Since we do not have an alternative. We do not have a proven economics model or theory so far for our current situations.

Do you know that concept of "conditional" is already proven in mathematics? In mathematics, we are using conditional probability, right? Conditional means already given situation.

In other words, I am talking about limitations here such as given that resources are running out, for example. Oil is running out in 30 years or so.

What will happen? What will become limitations? Most likely current airplane of jet engines will become unusable. We may be able to use gliders or balloons only instead, for example.

Although conditional economy itself has not be proven, it is just an addition of restrictions on free economy, and thus it should be fine or reasonably justifiable to use based on logical thinking.

I agree with you that conditional free economy in conjunction with conditional democracy will not be better than free economy with respect to economic prosperity and personal freedom. Free economy and democracy only works properly under healthy and normal conditions.

My point here is what will happen when conditions are off range? Can we really afford to free economy from now on even though it will not work properly under unhealthy and abnormal conditions? Our Environment has been changed as we are facing the climate change right now. Also it is obvious that there exist limitations such as scarce resources on the earth.

If we choose conditional free economy in conjunction with conditional democracy, we need to watch for a dictatorship such as that of Hitler's in the past.

This means as follows:

(On the condition that) When the public interests get hurt, somebody most likely the EARTH GOVERNMNNT intervenes it.

On the condition that the public interests get hurt, the EARTH GOVERNMNNT will set guidelines, regulations, or laws as necessary basis. The earth government must control monopolies with anti-monopoly laws and regulations.

As long as we find a way to prevent a dictatorship, conditional free economy in conjunction with conditional democracy should be fine since it is just a temporary application in-between from free economy to CIRCULAR ECONOMY.

Chapter 13. Economic Gains.

<Economic Gains>

Based on Adam Smith's "Wealth of the Nations", we will gain benefits from our economic activities (economic gains) mainly from the following factors:

1. Division of Labor:
2. Exchange of Surplus Produce
3. Economic Growth/ Expansion

1. Division of labor:
   Division of labor improves dexterity and helps to save time and thus it improves productivity and inevitably creates more output.
   If you have some doubt, please read "The Wealth of The Nations".

2. Exchange of Surplus Produce
   When we specialize in some part of a whole job, we inevitably produce more and often times more than we consume by ourselves because of improved dexterity, time-saving of switching, etc. BY exchanging surplus produce each other, we will have mutual benefits in a way of barter, commerce, and trade.
   Everybody wins by exchanging or conducting commerce.
   This is better explained in "the Wealth of Nations", of course because he is a genius.

3. Economic Growth/ Expansion:
   When excluding both division of labor and commerce in the above mentioned, economic activities will be a zero-sum game, which means that somebody gains at the expense of somebody else's loss proportionately, which is the case in a zero-sum game such as a game of Chinese mahjong. This means that the size of a pie stays the same and only distribution of its share changes.
   When economy grows, the size of the pie gets bigger and thus everybody gains from economic expansion.

This is the main reason that economists emphasize expansion and economic growth.

There are always pros and cons.
Economic growth also means we use or spend more resources than no growth situation.

Here we have a trade-off situation between economic growth and preservation of scarce resources.

It is estimated that we have enough coal for 118 years and oil for 30 years or so. Some resources such as gold and silver are less than for 20 years.

We have to think about these limitations as a trade-off for economic gains.

In other words, we can no longer afford to pursue the best scenario or option for maximizing economic gains such as using the current system. Instead, we need to choose the second best option such as sacrificing economic gains at the expense of our survival needs, namely, preservation of our species. In other words, give up and sacrifice economic efficiency and look for effectiveness instead. Abandon current efficiency model of economics and choose to switch to less efficient but effective second best economics model such as conditional free economy. Here I am talking about using minimum regulations on the condition that it hurts public interests such as overspending natural resources or consumption-driven current economy.

What are cons?

If we use regulations, price will go up somewhat and we will create some room for inefficiency as well as some inequalities.

That is why I am proposing to apply minimum interventions only on necessary basis.

Under the current circumstances of the U.S. economy with China, the U.S. needs to change its stance, for example.
In Rome, do as Romans do.
With China, do as Chinese government does.

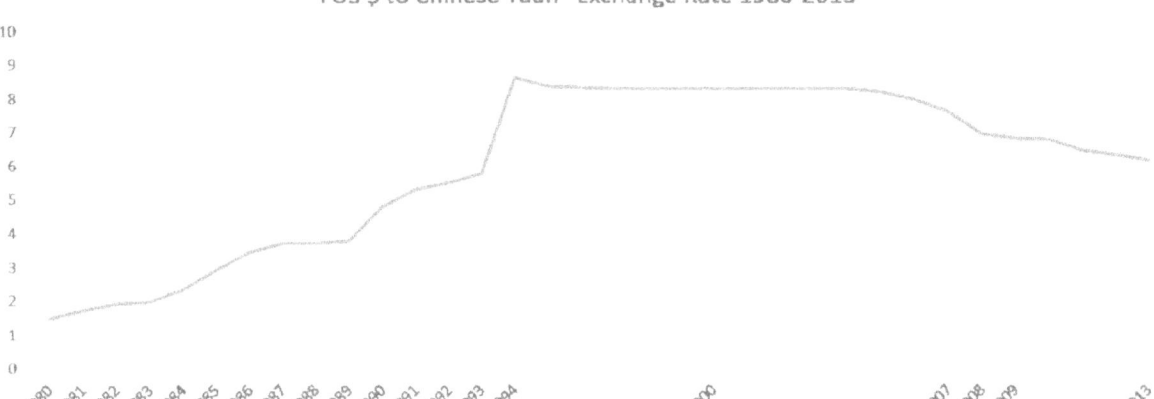

(Graph 29, Exchange Rate between US$ and Chinese Yuan.)

<Reconsideration of exchange rate between the U.S. $ and Chinese Yuan.>

Considering the Trade deficits of the U.S. with China, Chinese Yuan has to be stronger against the U.S. dollars. Which means that slope of the right side has to come down sharply such as 1$ = 3 Yuan or so in the above graph instead of staggering around 1$ = 6 or 7 Yuan or so based on the theory of free economy with free fluctuations of exchange rate when invisible hand is working.

The U.S. needs to use some forces with China because China uses more than enough interventions which have led to create accumulated trade deficits for the U.S. with China for the past thirty years or so. Self-adjusting mechanism such as free fluctuations of exchange rate has not been working due mainly to manipulations by Chinese government. Semi-fixed exchange rates between the U.S $ and Chinese Yuan was not good enough to offset the trade imbalance between the two as far as I can see from the history of exchange rates between the two.

For example, the U.S trade deficit has been increasing since 1985 up to the present very drastically.

If self-adjusting mechanism were working properly, Chinese Yuan would have gotten gradually stronger against the U.S. $, which did not happen at all in the past. Instead, movement or fluctuations of exchange rate between the two are very artificial, not natural. Since those are sudden ups and downs, which are not gradual nor natural, these must be clearly and intentionally managed by Chinese government when taking a look at historical graph of movements.

Chinese yuan was getting weaker until about 1994, while China has keep making trade surpluses to the U.S., which is contradictory to the theory of free trade.

After that, Chinese yuan got stronger against the U.S. $ somewhat, which was not good enough to adjust trade imbalance between China and the U.S. since the U.S. trade deficits keep continually increasing dramatically after 1994.

If the U.S. wants to clear the trade deficits with China by adjusting exchange rate alone, most likely we need to set exchange rate at about 2 Chinese yuan = 1 US $ or so which was the case before 1983 when the trade imbalance was very small between the two. By the way, it is currently about 6 Chinese yuan = 1 US $.

This is not unrealistic figures, though.

For example, back in very old days, exchange rate was fixed at 1 US $ = 360 Japanese Yen.

In these days, it is about 1 US $ = 120 Yen or so.

In the past, it went to 1 US $ = less than 80 Yen or so at peak.

In other words, the U.S. dollar was devalued by one third against Japanese Yen for the past 40 or 50 years or so.

China should be no exception in my opinion.

However, since Chinese economy is not free economy from the beginning, China will never give up a privilege/advantage of intervention. This is the way China handles its economy, namely controlled economy.

In other words, integer plus non integer equals non integer.

Integer + non integer = non integer.

When the U.S. engage with China economically, the rule of economy is not free economy. Instead it is already controlled economy with interventions (by Chinese government.)

Here concept of conditional free economy comes in.

In Rome, do as Romans do. With China, do as Chinese government does. We use free economy on the condition that it does not hurt the public interests or it is properly functioning.

On the condition when free economy or self-adjusting mechanism is not working well, we will use regulations or necessary means of interventions such as import duties etc.

For example, if we charge 10% import duties for all Chinese incoming goods from China to the U.S., it is the same thing as 10% adjustment of exchange rate between the U.S. $ and Chinese Yuan. Of course, exchange rate adjustment is better and a lot easier. However, when there is no other way, this might be the last option/resort in my opinion.

By the way, I am not recommending the above stated because it may lead to a block economy and thus it might lead to or cause a war in the end. Looking at the history of the WWII, this is the case.

Anyway, the U.S. definitely needs to clear up the trade deficit with China ASAP since it has left untouched for the past 30 years or so.

The U.S. free economy plus Chinese non-free economy equals de-facto non-free economy.

The U.S. Free economy + Chinese non-free economy = de-facto non-free economy.

In other words, self-adjusting mechanism will never work at non-free economy which has empirically proved in the past thirty years of experiences between the U.S. and Chinese trade results.

Accordingly, self-adjusting mechanism will never work in the future between the above two countries because the economic system is not free economy between the two.
If we use the same system/process, we will get the same result. The same system, the same result.
If we want to get a different result, we have to change the system/process.

Therefore, the U.S. needs to adjust it manually by herself such as suggesting the worst scenario unless China agrees to adjust the exchange rate such as valuation of Chinese yuan to the U.S. $ as much as two folds or three holds until the trade balance reaches to zero between the two.

Trade imbalance is just a symptom.
The real cause must be our life styles, habits, and the system.

Chapter 14. Change of our Life Styles.

In the meantime, I do recommend to change our life styles and our habits as follows:

1. Industry. Work hard.
2. Thrift.
3. Save money and invest.

The above three are main traits of wealth accumulators in the U.S. according to "The millionaire next door."
Only about 3.5% of population are millionaires in 1990's and have these traits accordingly.

<An Example from Benjamin Franklin>

"The Settlement of that Province had lately been begun; but instead of being made with hardy industrious Husbandmen accustomed to Labour, the only People fit for such an Enterprise, it was with Families of broken Shopkeepers and other insolvent Debtors, many of indolent and idle habits, taken out of the Goals, who being set down in the Woods, unqualified for clearing Land, and unable to endure the Hardships of a new Settlement, perished in Numbers, leaving many helpless Children unprovided for."("The Autobiography of Benjamin Franklin")

My understanding of the above sentence:
1. This project failed.
2. Reasons: indolent and idle habits.
   <Success factor >
   - Hardy industrious, instead.
   - Goals.

Could you see a similarity between this project and the U.S. conditions right now?

a. Broken, insolvent. V.S. 2007/2008 financial crisis.
b. Indolent and idle. V.S. couch potatoes.

According to Benjamin Franklin, we have to work hard and industrious and endure the hardship as a group instead of just one person' effort to be successful.

This happened about 250 years ago in the U.S.
If we do not change our habits, the same thing will happen again because people are the same American citizens or your ancestors. Only difference is time.

Under the democracy system, only a majority counts and thus over 50% of population in the U.S. need to have these traits.

The followings are the data I have.
<A Symptom V.S. A Cause>
A symptom: Huge national debts.
A Cause: Increased unproductive labor and decreased productive labor.

1. We have many holidays in the U.S. Holidays are classified as unproductive labor by Adam Smith.
2. A majority of people work 9 to 5 and take two days off per week. According to the bible, work 6 days a week and take one day off.

<A Symptom V.S. A Cause>
A symptom: Huge national debts.
A Cause: High consumption life styles.

3. Lots of people have high consumption life styles which are recommended by consumption driven economy. On the other hands, most wealth accumulators are thrift and they live below their means. Wealth accumulators save money and invest it. This is how capitalism works. Capital produce interests when invested because compound rate of interests grows exponentially.

Inversely, in case of many American people right now, they spend maximum amounts of money on credit which is borrowing. Compound rate of interests will kill them and thus this is the most efficient way to become poor in capitalism society, which is recommended by economists in the U.S. (Consumption driven economy.) This does not make sense to me. Surprise, surprise.

The U.S. Government is doing the same thing.

Trade deficits for the past 30 years or more.

As far as I checked, the U.S. has kept trade deficits since at least 1987 continuously. (Data Source: US Census Bureau.)

According to Trade economics, "The Unites States has been running consistent trade deficits since 1976 due to high imports of oil and consumer products." Actually I do not remember when the U.S. made trade surplus for a long time.

It means overspending. Financing it by borrowing.

The result is about 18 trillion $ of national debts in 2014 in the U.S.

Interest payment alone is about 0.43 trillion $.

We have to turn it around.

A majority of people need to become industrious, thrift, and money savers instead of a minority of people.

<A Symptom V.S. A Cause>
A symptom: Huge national debts.
A Cause: Surplus consumption.

GDP (what we produce) – Spending = Wealth or Debt
In the U.S. we have surplus consumption.

National Debt means that Spending > GDP (What we produce) as a nation.

Wealth accumulators: Income > Spending.

In other words, solutions for the national debts are as follows:

1. Spend less and save more money and invest it as wealth accumulators do. The majority of people as well as the U.S. government need to do it. Top 3.5% of population is millionaires and these people work hard, thrift, save money and invest it. I know that top managements and managers work very hard in the U.S. but they are only minorities in democracy. Lots of people are holiday-conscious rather than work-conscious. The majority of people need to become industrious and work-conscious rather than holiday-conscious in order to turn around the current economic situation in my opinion.
However, I do not blame on people. I only blame on the system. It must be very difficult to get a satisfying job in the U.S. since manufacturing jobs are mostly gone to China, for example. Our current business and economic system make us less enthusiastic about working hard because competition is not fair anymore. One of the reasons is monopolies. We have an issue of huge discrepancy of wealth or inequality of wealth thus we need to solve this issue together simultaneously.
2. Increase income or GDP. We have to increase productive labor first in order to produce more. We have to have enough surplus produce for exporting. After that, increase exports and reduce imports. Exchange rate adjustment by manually should help.
3. Change life styles and habits. We have to change our thinking or belief first before changing our behaviors. We can only spend to the extent what we produce. It is not the way around. First thing first. Production or make money first and spend it afterwards or later. We should honor productive labor and industry. We should take holidays sparingly since these are unproductive labor.
4. Consumption driven economy is not appropriate anymore. Consumption driven means that spend money first and pay it later, which is exactly what is happening right now. We spend money first as a nation by borrowing. What is the result? We accumulated the national debts of about 18 trillion $ which we have to pay for in the end. We have a choice of going on default which will definitely lead to a next great depression in the world. Under the current circumstances of scarce resources, we need to abandon consumption

driven economy and switch to moderate consumption economy, which means slowing down our economy and make somewhat economically stagnant even though nobody likes it in order to increase the chance of our survival in the years to come. We need to make sure to provide enough foods for poor people at the same time when economy gets stagnant because poor people will get hurt first.

<Learn from Adam Smith>
(Give reward after the work or production.)
(Production first, Consumption afterwards.)
(Opposite of consumption driven economy)

Adam Smith says in his book as follows:
"Public services are never better performed than when their reward comes only in consequence of their being performed, and is proportioned to the diligence employed in performing them."
From the above sentence, important points in my point of view are as follows:
- Reward afterwards and it should be proportional.
Since we need to evaluate their performance first, reward will be given to them proportionately after the work.
It means that work first and reward later, which is a natural cycle. We are doing the opposite right now. Reward or consumption first and payment later. No wonder we do not have enough motivation for getting rewards since rewards are already given in a way of consumption driven economy now.
- Diligence.
Idleness should not be rewarded.

<In the U.S. right now>
Reward first regardless of its performance. (Consumption first and payment later or postponement of payment for a very long time.)
(Technically speaking, no payment for more than the past 60 years thanks to ingenuity of economists.)

This is a reversed natural cycle. The cost is waiting for us, namely compound rate of interests.

Idleness could also be rewarded since reward is given first right now in the U.S.

Excess reward or surplus consumption for more than the past 60 years.

Diligent people are only minorities. Most diligent people are rich and affluent, though.

People work less when they get paid first or beforehand according to my psychological knowledge and hands-on experiences.

Chapter 15. A New Economics Model.

<A New Economics Model>

Here I am talking about simulation models for economics.

We can use current economics model just as a reference or an untested idea because it is violating the use instructions by ignoring limitations.

From now on, we need to use what if scenario such as follows:

1. What if we do not have oil anymore? What is the next best choice? Wind and solar energy can fully replace it?

   Right now, we will have serious issues on that because we are facing limitations such as scarce resources in addition to the Climate change derived from carbon emissions.

   My point here is that we can handle our situations without any economic growth because we can still gain a lot from the other two factors, which is division of labor and commerce based on Adam Smith's wisdom.

<Struggling middle classes in the U.S.>

There days I often read and hear about global middle classes.
On the contrary, in the U.S. middle classes are shrinking. One of my explanations are as follows:

<Lots of Factory jobs are gone from the U.S.>

As far as I remember, the U.S. companies started moving factories from the U.S. to Asia, mainly China since around 1990'.
In other words, the U.S. workers have lost lots of factory jobs since around 1990'. On the other hand, workers in Asia, mainly China gained substantial number of factory jobs. When Production goes up, Income goes up. I tend

to believe that global middle classes were created by production outsourcing trends by global companies.

Chapter 16. Dysfunctional U.S. Economy.

Consumer driven economy is not functioning well within a frame work of the U.S.

<Economic Cycle in theory.>

There is an economic cycle between production (+) and consumption (-).

We can only consume (-) what we produce (+) in nature.

Since the U.S. economists inversed the natural cycle, we consume first and production later based on consumption driven economy.

When Consumption goes up, Production goes up. When Production goes up, Income goes up. When Income goes up, Consumption goes up.

This is the healthy economic cycle which works perfectly in theory or as long as the basic assumptions are not violated.

<In the U.S., since economic cycle is incomplete, economic cycle is dysfunctional.>

(Violation of the Use Instructions.)

In the U.S., when Consumption goes up, Production may or may not goes up. Since there aren't many productions in the U.S. anymore, Production goes up very slightly. When Production goes up very slightly, Income goes up very slightly. When Income goes up very slightly, (Consumption would go up very slightly in theory.) In other words, economic cycle is dysfunctional within a frame of the U.S.

<From here, stimulation of consumption by the U.S. government.>

In order to stimulate economy or consumption, the U.S. government makes every possible efforts which you know.

- Governmental spending. Public spending creates jobs.

- Lowering taxes. This stimulates consumption.

When all productions were conducted in the U.S., for example, the U.S. government would not need to do anything at all because economic cycle would take care of it.

(A symptom: Stagnant income growth of middle classes.)

(A real cause: Job loss mostly factory jobs to Asia, mainly China.)

Since the followings are statistical data, we need to consider at least 5% of deviations or so.

However, this is consistent with Gini statistic of the United States such that rich people got richer and poor people got poorer. It looks like that middle income households are also still suffering since 2007/2008 financial crisis. Middle Class's Income level of after 2007/2008 crisis are roughly the same level of about 20 years ago.

<Real Middle Class Income is not growing in the U.S.>

1995	52,604($)
1996	53,345
2007	57,357
2008	55,313
2013	52,789
2014	53,675

(Data Source: statista.com)

Actually income level of middle class is lower now than that of 2007/2008 level. This is one of a sign that the United States economy has not been fully recovered since 2007/2008 financial crisis.

By the way, considering inflation rate, the same amounts means actually a decline in real value. $53,000 of 20 years ago is not the same as $53,000 now. Suppose inflation rate is 2% in average, $(1+0.02)^{20}$ is 1.48. $53,000 of money 20 years ago worth more than $78,000 of money now. Oh my god, this is about 32% decline of income in real value now compared with that of 20 years ago. (78K-53K/78K) No wonder that the U.S. people talk about suffering of middle income range. In other words, middle class was better off 20 years ago than now.

Have you noticed that global companies started lots of productions in China since around early 1990's? By 1995, there weren't many productions in the U.S. anymore as far as I remember. In other words, with globalization trend, the U.S. economy started more and more dysfunctional as more and more factory jobs were taken away from the U.S. workers based on my observations.

Income lever decline from 2007/2008 to 2013/2014 also shows another indication that the United States' economy has not been fully recovered yet.

Most likely middle class households are suffering from domestic job losses due mainly to the United States' out-sourcing and off-shore manufacturing trend such as making China as manufacturing-hub for the U.S. since early 1990's.

<A Symptom V.S. A Cause>

(A symptom: Almost no growth of real middle class income.)

(A Cause: Manufacturing Job loss to China.)

(A Root Cause: The last man standing game of the current business system.)

If we do not out-source manufacturing to China, somebody else will. This is a fear based action.

Since the U.S. has enough debts already now, we can no longer afford this kind of consumption driven economy in my opinion.

Chapter 17. Change Economic System.

From Max spending to Min Losses.
Max Spending = Consumption driven economy.
Min Losses = Circular Economy in the end.

Suppose consumption driven economy is maximizing spending model, I am talking about minimizing losses model.

What does it mean?

Right now we are wasting lots of foods, energies, and materials. If we minimize these losses, we can still create a room for growth a little bit.

<Mundane Examples>

For example, lots of printed books are wasted without being read/bought when publishing new paper books.
We can minimize losses with combination of e-books, print-on-demand, and normal paper books, for example. By reducing the volume of one batch volume of paper books unless it is absolutely sure to sell them out, we can go from either e-books or print-on-demand or both in the beginning.
This is already happening. I am just giving you a simple example.
When we change our system, people will come up with good ideas in order for adjusting changed conditions/environments. That is why it is very important for us to change our systems right now.

In business when sales goes down we have to cut expenses accordingly. In a household when income goes down we have to cut spending also. But in economy when everybody stops spending we will have a recession/deflation/depression and thus a government needs to facilitate economy by every means including public spending in order to prevent a depression and promote some inflation, for example.

This is an economic theory as a whole so far.

But wait a minute. I have some concern with it.
Please note that I am talking about a bird-eye point of view here.
Due mainly to global or the Earth economy now, can the U.S. government function as the Earth government?
No, at least based on jurisdiction.
It makes sense to me that if the Earth government goes on to public spending on world-wide instead of the U.S. government goes on to public spending in the U.S. independently.

My point here is as follows:
We need to have the Earth government to take care of total or overall P/L statements of the earth since the economy is already global. The U.S. economy per se is already dysfunctional due mainly to globalization of economy right now. The current economics theory will be better fit when it is applied by the earth government on earth basis.
Since we do not have the Earth government yet, nobody controls P/L statement as a whole right now. In other words, unless we apply the current economics theory on the earth basis, it will not work as it promises. For example, the U.S. economy is dysfunctional now based on my observations.

Chapter 18. Additional Information.

<Additional Information/reference>

The U.S. GDP represents about 22.5% of world GDP.
(Data Source: Sekaino Keizai Netachou in Japanese, data on internet)
(17,418.93 billion $ / 77,301.96 billion $)

The U.S. population represents about 4.4% of world population.
(321 million/7,349 million) (Data Source: United Nations 2015)

<Concept of product life cycle>
In business, concept of life cycle is a must thing to know. No body grows forever. There is a cycle of introduction, growth, maturity, and decline.
This is also true with human beings. Infant, child, youth, maturity/adult, and elder.

Of course, there exists so called a parachute effect (the second time growth opportunity) when another/new usage was discovered. However, eventually, everything is subjected to stop growing or stationary, and declining.

<Diffusion model of Frank Bass> (Marketing Models)
This model is very useful for predictions of future sales or market potentials of durable commodities based on the first several years of sales data for commodities such as TV, radio, refrigerator, etc.
This means that these commodities have similar life cycle patterns and thus it is highly predictable.
There exist cycles of life. Everything is subject to stop growing and declining in the end.
Commodities will reach to its saturation in a highly predictable pattern.
In other words, there always exist limitations in business and real world where economists still assume no limitations in theory. Do we have some misunderstandings here? Who is living in a fantasy land? Economists or us?

<Competitive Destruction> (Charles T. Munger):
 "Today only one, General Electric, remains business as a large, independent company" (Fifty most important stocks then (in 1911), actively traded on the New York Stock Exchange.)
1/50 = 2 % of survival rate at the New York Stock Exchange.

In other words, only 2% survived and 98% have been gone in the past about 100 years on the New York Stock Exchange listings.

I would say that General Electric is an exception.
In other words, GE has been continuously grown and met the requirements of the expansion model.
Probably, General Electric has managed to grow for the past 100 years including mergers and acquisitions. When a company stops growing, the company will be thrown out, or becoming a target for mergers and acquisitions.

In my opinion, our life on the earth has reached to maturity stage and thus expansion model or expecting ever growing economy is not suitable or unfit. When we are young, we want to eat as much as possible. When our stomachs are full, we are satisfied. This is similar to consumption driven economics model, which encourages consumer to spend/consume as much as possible.

When we get older, we do not need to eat so much. We prefer to eat smaller quantity of better quality food to satisfy our needs. We become quality-oriented instead of volume-conscious when we get older.
The same should be true with our economics model.
We should switch from consumption driven economy to more quality oriented economics model.
What does this mean?
I am sorry but I do not have a clear answer for it. All I can say is as follows:
- Do not promote or push consumption too much. Give up consumption-driven economy.
- Do not waste natural resources including foods.

- Facilitate on-demand productions. Stop looking for only efficiency because we can produce things cheaper but at the same time we will create lots of losses.
- Sharing (car sharing, for example.)
- Shifting emphasis on re-cycling such that Ms. Ellen McArthur is saying.

Chapter 19. Industry Driven Economy.

<Industry Driven Economy>

What I am proposing is so to speak Industry driven economy.
The cycle of economy is the same as the natural cycle.
Production first by industrious people. Here we will lose some selections or choice by consumers. We may have to produce from what available for us and minimizing losses. In other words, we will be producing things similar to uniforms of baseball players, for example.
When Production goes up, Employment goes up and Income goes up.
When Income goes up, Consumption goes up. When Consumption goes up, Production goes up. Here we create a healthy economic cycle from production to consumption.

Chapter 20. Population Management.

<Manage Population Growth>

A Symptom: The Climate Change.
A Real Cause: Population growth.

Our current issues are also something to do with population growth.
When the population grows, we spend and consume more and thus emit more CO_2 accordingly.
As economy grows, population will grow inevitably because of increased subsistence.

World population is est. 7.3 billion in 2015. (PRB's population projections)

2011	7 billion
1998	6 billion
1987	5 billion
1974	4 billion
1961	3 billion
1927	2 billion
1802	1 billion

(Data Source: Angus Maddison and Wikipedia on internet combined.)

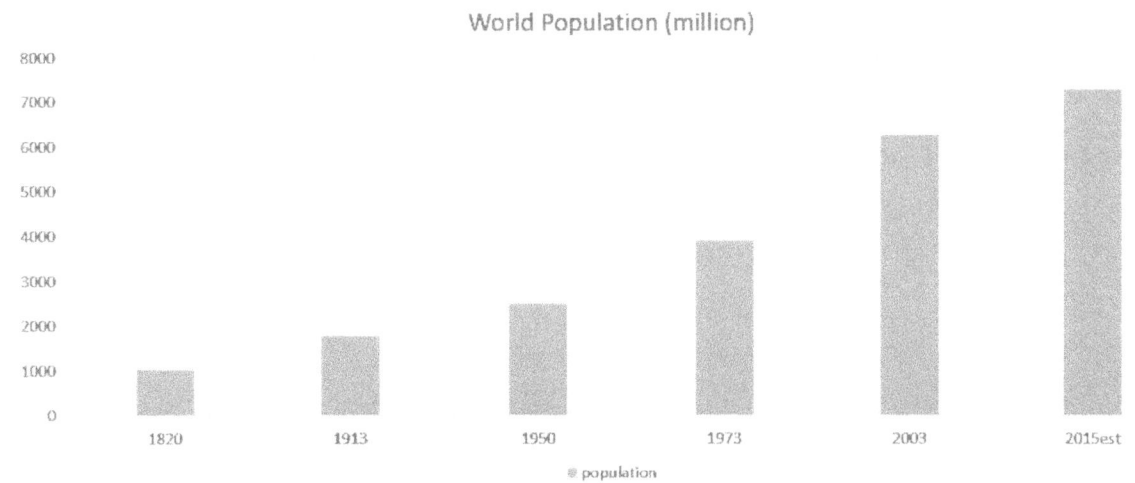

(Graph 30, Population growth. Data Source: Angus Maddison, etc.)

By the way, according to Adam Smith, Population grows to the extent of subsistence.

Some expert predicts that world population will grow up to 10 billion. According to PRB's population projections in the 2015 data sheet, "world population will be reaching 9.8 billion by 2050."
On the other hand, according to Mr. Richard Branson, affordable population on earth is estimated about 5 billion by scientists.

Unfortunately in human history, we have never been successful managing population growth.
Population was managed by calamities such as wars, famines, and diseases in the past.
I am in favor of contraceptives.
CO_2 tax being proposed by Mr. Ale Gore may work.
Poll tax may work.
In the end, we humans are intrinsically animals whose reproduction urge is inherent/embedded and thus it must be really hard to control population growth.

<Stop Population Growth>

Since it is basically impossible for us to reduce population, we should avoid increasing population further. As economy grows, population will grow inevitably because of increased subsistence. In other words, if we want to slow down population growth, we may need to slow down our economy too. In this sense, consumption driven economy is self-killing and thus we have to abandon it.

Based on Mr. Richard Branson's information, affordable population on earth is estimated about 5 billion people by the scientists. We have already exceeded this number by 30 % or so.

According to Adam Smith, population grows to the level of subsistence. In this respect, we should avoid outsourcing manufacturing to developing countries, for example. It will increase subsistence in mainly Asia and thus population in Asia will grow further.

We may want to give disincentives for manufacturing outsourcing such as follows:

 - Charge poll taxes to the company when shifting or having shifted factories to developing countries based on the number of employees hired as a consequence. Use this poll taxes only for the Climate Change project such as planting trees, shifting to solar and wind energies, etc. We definitely need to form an earth government for this kind of conduct.

Chapter 21. Impact of the Climate Change.

<Impact of the Climate Change>

"It is predicted that global temperature will increase by 6 degrees (11 degrees F); each one degree C increase in temperature is expected by expert to produce a 10 percent decline in crops yields" ("The Future", Al Gore)

I have no comment on this because this is just a prediction.
However, we will be in a bad shape as far as food supply is concerned in the future. Do we want to let the population grow to the extent of subsistence which Adam Smith is saying based on his logic?

Let's see, we have 7.3 billion people now. Population will reach 9.8 billion by 2050, which is 34 % increase.

Let suppose, temperature increase by 4 degrees C, which is 40 % decrease in crops.

Let set Current level to be 1.

Population will be 1.34.
Crops will be 0.6.

0.6 / 1.34 = about 0.45.

Foods will be available for about 45% of current level in 2050.
We will be hungry but we can still survive since we are wasting lots of foods right now and we are taking too much calories anyway now.

But is this what we want in the future?

Can we take a proactive action early enough in order to avoid pains and difficulties in the future?

Chapter 22. Summaries.

<Summaries>

1. Current economic and business models are unfit for the current changed conditions. We need to change our system for adjusting to changed environments. We can no longer afford consumption driven economy. We may want to change them to conditional economy before moving to CIRCULAR Economy.
2. The U.S. has huge national debts as much as about $18 trillion and financing by borrowing is no longer appropriate considering huge amounts of interest payments such as $0.43 trillion a year. The U.S. needs to make ends meet ASAP. In other words, we may need to use both conditional economy and conditional democracy for achieving this objective
3. Alleviation of symptoms such as money supply expansion will no longer well enough nor continue to be effective. And thus, we may need to work on fundamental causes for curing such as follows:
   1. Increase what we produce by changing our Life Styles and habits. Apply Industry driven economy. Increase productive labor and decrease unproductive labor.
   Be thrift. Spend less than what we produce. In other words, make our ends meet. Obtain a saving habit. Change from current spending habit to saving habit. Only a minority of people, most of them are rich in the U.S. have saving habits as far as I know. Here democracy comes in. Under democracy system, a majority counts, numbers count, quantity counts.

Democracy only works well in peace and healthy conditions because it relies on people's healthy conducts such as logical thinking and logical behaviors.
Human beings make good and logical decisions in peace and healthy conditions.
On the contrary, when panic, emergency, or war like situation, human beings act illogically like animals such as stealing and killing, or whatever takes for our survival. In other words, we act illogically and do not make good/logical decisions under unhealthy and abnormal conditions.

Therefore, democracy will not work properly or function well in abnormal, unhealthy, or panic conditions.

By the same token, when a majority of people have spending habits, all decisions will be affected and thus all decisions will be pro-spending now. You see now we are trying to make our ends meet but a majority of people are pro-spending. What will happen? When it comes to vote or democratic decisions, opinions of spenders' (or bad habit possessors') always become dominant. Thrifty persons' or good habit possessors' opinions in abnormal conditions under the democracy never win because a majority of opinion count. In other words, quantity kills quality. This is why we may need to change our habits and life styles of a majority of people from over-spending to thrift and pro-saving until these become a majority. In the meantime, we may want to use conditional democracy when emergency situation or abnormal conditions exist such as right now. Here I am talking about Conditional. In this case it is free on the condition that it does not hurt the public interests. The public interest here is to payback the national debts ASAP in order to avoid going to defaults, which will lead to a disaster such as another great depression, most likely.

Nobody likes to take pains. An Earth government should help the U.S. government to take pains in this case in my opinion. Besides, when we have the earth government, it should be able to work as a buffer to absorb some chaos if and only if the U.S. government become insolvent. On the national level, the U.S. needs to make the trade balance break-even or positive ASAP. For this purpose, the U.S. needs to make the trade balance with China to break-even or positive ASAP because it represents about 68% of the Trade deficits for the U.S. these days. We could adjust exchange rate between the U.S. $ and Chinese yuan. Or the U.S. can impose purpose specific duties to all importing Chinese products excluding foods, for example, although this is none of my business though as long as the U.S. will not go on defaults. This duty tax income should be only used for paying back debts to China, for example because its purpose is balancing the trade imbalance only.

Conclusion:

In conclusion, what I am trying to say are as follows:

I. Create an Earth Government
II. Create an Earth Money (Cyber Money)
III. Abandon Consumption driven economy. Use Industry driven economy. Apply Economics theory on the earth basis.
IV. Use New Business Systems. Min Growth or No growth model.
V. Apply New Mind-sets and New Life Styles. Benjamin Franklin Campaign.
VI. Re-booting or re-starting our economy.

I. Necessity of an Earth Government.

Right now several critical factors for our prosperity and wellness are unmanaged because we do not have a proper institution to control or govern those. Without creating an earth government, we will never be able to control or manage our critical situations such as population growth and economic expansion race on earth, etc. for example.

Since we have severe limitations right now on the contrary to the no limitation assumption of our economics theory, we have to manage our activities somehow accordingly.

Here we have at least two things to consider as follows:

<Our Survival needs. Preservation of natural resources.>

A. Wrong application of economics model on completely changed environments right now. Assumption of no limitations are clearly unmet right now. In other words, we are severely violating the use instructions of economics theory and thus we are no longer sure whether consumption driven economy is our best choice or not. Actually we must be insane if we want to keep using consumption driven economy from now on since we will be using up natural resources as quickly and efficiently as possible. This is a danger of applying economics theory while violating its assumptions such as abundant resources and no limitations. We can no longer afford consumption driven economy given that natural resources are running out such as oil and coals. Industry driven economy is recommended instead.

<Violation of the Use Instructions.>

(Dysfunctional Current Economy.)

    B. Inappropriate application of economics model per se.
    First of all, it is wrong to apply pure and mathematical economics models on our real world when basic assumptions are severely violated such as now.
    In other words, we are violating use instructions of economics theory. Saying it differently, use instructions say that do not use the theory where there exist limitations, etc. since the theory will not work as it promises.
    Secondly, due mainly to globalization of current economies, it is more appropriate and wise to apply and govern our economies as a single unit, that is, on the earth basis. The current economics theory is only true when applied on a single and confined market.
    In other words, it will not work properly otherwise. These days, since our economy is highly global and this condition is severely violated, economics theory will never work properly as it promises in the real global world.

<Necessity of establishing an Earth Government. >

    Only way to make it workable is to apply it on the earth basis in order to make it confined.
    All in all, current economy is uncontrollable without having any proper executive power as a whole, which will be an earth government.
    We have to control monopolies at least, which are one of major causes of dysfunctional economy right now.
    However, it must be extremely difficult to establish an Earth Government, which is non-existent in our human history. Although we have the United

Nations, its position is below or under the individual government. I tend to believe that the United Nations have no power over economic issues right now. One of the reasons must come from lack of income generating system or sources such as tax revenues.

Any government needs income sources such as tax revenues to run for it.

<Income Source for an Earth Government.>

As I see the way it is, every government lives or relies on taxes as its major income source. The earth government needs to collect taxes. For this purpose, I propose the following taxes to begin with:

A. CO_2 tax. Actually this is Mr. Gore's idea, though. This works as a disincentive for free spending of fossils based on consumption-driven economy.

B. Population tax or poll tax.
I learned this from Adam Smith's book.
As you can see, we have to control both CO_2 level and population growth. Although population control is almost impossible based on our animal nature, we should at least try it because a real and fundamental cause of CO_2 Emission increase is population increase as you are aware of it.

Under the current circumstances, it may be easier and more implementable for us to combine the United Nations and G20 on cyber or on internet. In other words, we may want to create a cyber Earth Government on internet first by joint venture or joint system of the two. We also need a new earth money on internet, which will be similar or exactly the same as Bit Coins for purpose of world-wide-transactions. It is too dangerous to use US$ for this purpose. If and only if the United States goes on defaults, the money itself become insolvent. It is safer for us to create a new cyber earth money on internet and it will work as a buffer for chaotic situation when the U.S.'s condition gets worse.

II. An Earth Government Cyber Money.
We need to have free circulating money without any restrictions on the Earth basis when we apply our economy on the Earth as a single unit. If the

Erath Government takes over Bit Coins, for example, it must be very easy. However, for an ethical reason, I do not know how to justify it. May be we can borrow the concept and issue cyber money of the Earth Government and start using it on internet. By the way, it is also easier for us to start the Earth Government on internet, which is cyber Earth Government. I do not know how to proceed it and thus we have to consult it with experts or authorities about it. Since the Bit Coins did it, we can do it too.

III. New Economics Simulation Models.
Although we can apply conventional economics models on the Earth Economy governed by the Earth Government without any problem, we still need new economics simulation models in transitory periods as follows:
   A. Change assumptions from abundant resources to limited resources.
   B. Change assumptions from no limitations to step by step limitations, etc. We can set limitations and imagine it in our heads as long as we have a couple of variables to consider.
   When things get more complicated, we may have to program and apply limitations one by one based on some scenarios, most likely simulation models, such as follows:

   What if we run out of coals in 118 years from now and substitute it with solar and wind energy? Obviously we have to narrow down our choices further such as follows:

a.) Let it be. Status quo. Take no action. All free. Free economy as it is. No population control.
b.) Find a middle point and gradually control to a targeting point. Let's say that cut the consumption of coal by half in 59 years and replace it with solar and wind energy. Control population less than current level, let's say that less than 6 billion people in 59 years. This means about 10% decrease of population in 60 years or so and it must be about 0.2% decrease of population per year which should be achievable in my opinion.
c.) Strictly control both CO_2 emissions and populations by the Earth Government.

Let's say reduce number of populations to more ideal level such as 5 billion people where the scientists calculated as affordable. Switch to circular economy in 30 years or so.

We can go through simulations in our heads when we have only few variables. Can you see that it is a bad idea for us to keep using free economy system as it is and use up resources as fast as possible or as about 7.3 billion people wish? We are doing it right now. We have to change it because our current system such as economics model of free economy is unfit for unhealthy and emergency situations such as now. Here I am recommending conditional free economy and conditional democracy at marginally emergency conditions such as now. Conditional means limitations and controlling on necessary basis when only the public interests get hurt.

<A Pitfall of Democracy.>

Democracy only counts number, a majority of people, sheer quantity while ignoring quality. We may want to add quality of opinion as well and thus I am recommending as follows:

<Add Expert's opinion for quality.>

1. Create a panel of experts and come up with a couple of recommendations. All recommendations must be theoretically solid or must be sane.
2. We either vote for it or choose one of them somehow when quality lacking democracy leads us to silly decisions or conducts such as too extremes or obviously non-desirable ones. For example, increase unproductive labor and decrease productive labor up to the point where a government become nearly insolvent or going to bankrupt. Obviously we have to balance the budget in a way of decreasing unproductive labor and increasing productive labor even though the majority of people want more holidays and leisure. The majority of opinion always win under the democracy and this kind of thing never implemented under the democracy. Pure democracy is dis-functional now and needs to be rectified in this kind of current semi-emergency situations. In other words, unfortunately we have to work more and reduce holidays to the point where we can reach to the equilibrium or

balance the budget. Why did this happen? Because it is human and natural nature to maximize economic well beings. In other words, ideal situation for us as human beings is that we can get as much as we want without working for it at all. Therefore, unless we have a system to manage it somehow, it is inevitable for us to have this kind of situation in the long run or in the end. This is our human nature and thus it is a pitfall or fault of our system in my opinion.

<Change economic System>

<From consumption driven economy to industry driven economy.>

We can no longer afford consumption driven economy.
Actually, it is the worst choice for us when facing with deprivation of natural resources such as oil and coals right now.
Even thinking in a more economical sense, this is not a good idea in the long run or in the end. For example, spending money first (consumption-driven economy) by borrowing, we just postponed the timing of payment, that is all. We still have to pay for it in the end in a more painful manner in the long run as follows:

<Golden rules of nature>
1. What we produce, we can consume. This is a golden rule of thumb in this order. We can't consume until we produce in nature.
2. Production (+)= Consumption (-)
3. In Nature, production first and consumption next or later.
4. Production (+) > Consumption (-).
5. Conversely, when Consumption (-) > Production (+), we create debts.
   Over Consumption = Production (GDP) + Debt.
   If we want to reduce Debt, we need to have surplus produce, gain, or profit. In other words, we have to produce positive cash flows, which is trade surplus as a country of course.
   When Production > Consumption, we create a gain or profit. (Trade Surplus)

Since the United States has about $18 trillion of national debts now, if we want to reduce it, we can either increase what we produce(Production) or reduce Consumption or most likely we need to do both.

<Make our ends meet.>
In case of trade balance, it is as follows:

When Exports (+) < Imports (-)
Imports (-) > Exports (+) = Trade deficits (negative right now)

Firstly, we have to make the Trade balance positive, which means that we need to increase exports, reduce imports, or do both. Can you see that? Reduce imports means that we need to reduce consumptions, obviously. In other words, we are over-spending right now or we are consuming more than we produced. Why is that? This is induced by Consumption driven economy, right? We have to pay for it from now on before we go insolvent, even though an American doctor, M.D. mentioned that it will take 4700 years to pay back this much debt based on his assumptions and calculations. This is democracy, right? However, this is definitely an option in my opinion considering a consequence of going for defaults.

This is rather painful because we have to pay for the interest with compound rate, which is a torture. This is called Capitalism as far as I learned in the U.S. This is the first concerns in business or when constructing a business plan such as how much money do we have to borrow and whether it is justifiable or not? Capital or money creates interests. In other others, money makes money in Capitalism. The opposite is also true. A Debt creates more debts in Capitalism. Compound rate of interests are exponential and thus it starts giving accelerating effects/impacts with time going by. If we do not pay back the principal amounts, it will become more than doubled in the 30 years or so.

<Danger of compound interest rate>

$(1+r)^x$

Let's say interest = r = 3%

Number of years = x = 30 years.

$(1 + 0.03)^{30} = 2.427...$

This is exactly happening right now in the United States. As far as I checked, the United States has had trade deficits since 1953 or earlier, which is for the past 60 years or so. Unless a country produce trade surplus, the country can't pay back debts internationally.

<Violation of the assumption of economics theory>

<It is true within a confined market condition.>

By the way, a basic assumption of current economics theory or single unit theory is that the government borrows money within a market unit or in domestic market only.

Borrower=government V.S. Lenders=public.

Here a borrower and lenders are ultimately the same because the public owns the government and there is no problem in economics theory in this context.

In reality or the real world, it is not true, anymore. Because the United States is borrowing lots of money from the other foreign governments such as 6 trillion $ in total for example, by issuing Treasury Bonds, etc., the following two factors bothered us.

<Major foreign holders of treasury securities.>

(In billion dollars)(Aug 2015)

China, Mainland	1270.5
Japan	1197.0
Carib Bkg Ctrs 4/	329.0
Oil Exporters 3/	293.2
Grand Total	6098.7

(Data Source: treasury.gov)

In other words, 6 trillion $ of treasury securities are held by the other foreign governments, which are debts from the U.S. government's point of view.

6 trillion $ / 18 trillion $ = about 1/3.

About 1/3 of debts come from the outside of the U.S.

1. A Borrower and lenders are not the same.
   The U.S. government borrows money and the other governments lends roughly 33% of money in total such as China and the other foreign governments, etc.
2. Compound rate of interests are actually outflows of money or a bleeding, which is a loss of capital and thus it is bad in reality.
   On the contrary, based on the assumptions of a confined market economics theory, money including compound rate of interests circulates within a unit or in the U.S. and thus we have no problem, which is not true anymore in the real world.

By the way, consumption driven economy is great in terms of economic prosperity since consumption first acts like an accelerator for the economy. Which is first, a Chicken or an Egg? Which is first Production or Consumption? In Nature, Production first but it works as a constraint. When we change the order, and when we consumer first, it will act as an accelerator because a constraint is taken away to the extent where we can borrow. This is the invention of clever economists, right?

When we go back to original order or nature's cycle, Production comes first. And also Production has to be larger than Consumption in order to pay back debts. Why am I recommending it? Because I am not talking about economic prosperity only here. We have an emergency situation or survival needs here right now. As a result, I am talking about a) increasing our chance of survival and b) avoiding another World Great Depression when the U.S. becomes insolvent. In other words, I am recommending to sacrifice economic prosperity for the sake of preservation of resources as well as avoiding an economic disaster in the future. Yes, I am recommending a big change and change almost everything including business systems and our life styles, etc. The same system/process, the same result. If we change rules of the game, everything will be changed accordingly. Since rules of the game are defined by the system, we have to change our systems to better fit for emergency or limited resources situations of the coming future.

IV. A New Business System. (We cannot afford Consumption driven economy anymore.)

<Control Monopolies.>
<Monopolies make markets unhealthy.>
Under the current business system and economic system, it is well known that monopolistic conditions will be created in the end, let's say 20 to 30 years later after de-regulations, for example. According to Mr. Munger that there always survive 5 or 6 companies only in a market. I have seen monopoly model in micro economics class at UCR. In other words, when we leave it under the free competition, it will create a monopolistic condition in the end, which is theoretically or mathematically proven a long time ago. Everybody knows it. Anti-monopoly laws and regulations were effective until 20 or 30 years ago until our economy became global. In my opinion, right now anti-monopoly laws and regulations imposed by an each conventional government are not enforceable enough to prevent monopolistic conditions on global markets. As companies gets bigger and bigger globally and our market conditions get more and more uncontrollable. In other words, only big global companies or so called earth companies are reaping monopolistic benefits and killing the rests.

<Food chains>
(Natural Cycles)
There exist cycle of food chains. Planktons are eaten by small fishes. Small fishes are even by bigger fishes. Big fishes are eaten by even bigger fishes. When only gigantic fishes are left without smaller ones, food chains will be

broken. There will be no more foods available for gigantic fishes and eventually all gigantic fishes will die.

When gigantic fishes start struggling for foods, the situations will become very nasty. Right now we are economically experiencing this. As Earth companies are struggling for more expansion and more profits, these companies are tempted to exercise monopolistic powers and start creating lots of mess right now. We have to enforce anti-monopoly laws and regulations but we are not successful because we do not have an earth government to control earth companies unfortunately.

Actually companies are competing for getting bigger by M& A's, mergers and acquisitions. This is not a healthy state. Adam Smith also mentions in his book as follows:

"If but one of overgrown manufactures, which by means either of bounties or of monopoly of the home and colony markets, have been artificially raised up to an unnatural height, finds some small stop or interruption in its employment, it frequently occasions a mutiny and disorder….. " ("The Wealth of the nations", 1776.)

Adam Smith criticizes both bounties and monopoly in the above.

In other words, bounties (regulations) will create unnatural state, which is bad. => Perfect freedom or free economy is better.

On the other hand, monopoly is also bad for the same reason. => We have to prevent monopoly by any means.

<Restrictions of M&As >
(Easy and unnatural way to create monopolies.)

In my opinion, M&A should be restricted. M&As create monopolies very quickly and efficiently. M&As are last resorts for growth/ expansion and thus these have been abused right now in my opinion.

M&A's for the sake of getting bigger should be restricted by anti-monopoly laws, which is not functioning well on global market now.

We need an Earth Government to control monopolies in global market. Also we need an equivalent of warm boot-up system for personal computers, which is re-booting of our economies. Opposite of M&A's which is dividing or breaking down companies into two or three pieces should be an option. For example, Yusei or Yusei-kousha, a Japanese government owned corporation, was divided into three companies when going to the public or privatized in Japan. This was one method of preventing monopoly in the market, although it was strongly suggested by the U.S. as far as I know.

This is both good and bad. Every action has both pros and cons. It lost efficiency but instead we prevented a monopoly.

We have to do this kind of thing globally by the Earth Government based on fair judgement in order to secure fair and healthy competitions in the market. Where there exist monopolies, the market become dull, stagnant, or no competition because monopolies dominate everything and enjoy their monopolistic positions in the market.

Who created these problems? We did. Humans are only creatures who engage in economic activities on this planet. We as consumers asked for those. Economists and legislators responded them by making systems based on our requests. We wanted and asked more economic prosperity, cheaper goods, more leisure, and less work, etc.

Since we asked for those, economists came up with an idea of consumption-driven economy by borrowing money, etc.

V. New Mindsets and New Life Styles. Benjamin Franklin Campaign.
    <Fundamental Changes>
    We need to change ourselves fundamentally.
    In order to avoid a future disaster, we need to change our mindsets and life styles accordingly.

    From indolent and idle to industrious and hard working.

    From spending to saving.

    From couch potatoes to hardy industrious workers.

    a) Abandon Consumption driven economy. We can no longer afford consumption driven economy by spending lavishly because resources are limited. In other words, consumption-driven economy is no longer appropriate for us. We should go back to a natural state which is an equilibrium between Production and Consumption. Yes, we need to reduce consumptions gradually to the point where we naturally meet to what we produce. We have to stop over-consumption and thus we need to change our mindsets as follows:

- We are no longer rich in terms of natural resources and thus we have to save or preserve these in a reasonable degree. We will keep abundant mentality only. Keeping abundant mentality is very important for us. Otherwise, we will be mentally depressed. We will mentally think that there are enough resources for us but we will not spend them lavishly. We will save resources as much as possible. Yes, we will suffer economically but we can increase our probability of avoiding an economic disaster as well as our survival.

b) Change our Life Styles.

From idle and indolent to thrift and industry.

From intemperance to temperance.

Adam Smith says as follows:

"In the political body, however, the wisdom of nature has fortunately made ample provision for remedying many of the bad effects of folly and injustice of man, in the same manner as it has done in the natural body for remedying those of his sloth and intemperance."

In my opinion, the followings are important points:

- The wisdom of nature.

- Bad effects of sloth and intemperance.

("The Wealth of the Nations".)

BY the way, total sum of individual performance (what one produce) is GDP (what we produce) as a nation.

You see, when lots of people become sloth and intemperance, GDP will inevitably suffer or deteriorate.

What our economists are saying?

Consume more = Consumption driven economy.

What the government is saying?

Take more holidays (work less) and enjoy your life.

What companies are offering?

All you can eat and all you can drink.

What consumers are doing?

Oh yeah.

Eat and drink as much as possible= Intemperance.

Take many holidays (increase unproductive labor.) = Idleness.

What is the outcome?

One become idle and intemperance and thus produce less.

When lots of people become idle and intemperance, what we produce as a whole, or GDP will go down. This is exactly what is happening right now.

What should we do?

Both Benjamin Franklin and Adam Smith say based on the nature's wisdom as follows:

Temperance, frugality, and industry, right?

What is wrong? Why is this happening?

Our current system must be unfit for the current situation, right?

<Industry>

Increase quantity of productive labor and decrease quantity of unproductive labor such as holidays gradually. Up until now, we have been increasing quantity of unproductive labor which must be overdone based on accumulation of national debts in the past in the U.S.

Increase Production or what we produce first and place consumption next or afterwards. We have to make our ends meet at every level such as the Government and households, etc. We will give up our borrowing habits and we will not spend first. Instead, we will make money first or Production first.

Making China as a production hub is not economically wise because it is a loss of domestic employment.

This is just taking up jobs from American workers and giving jobs to Chinese people instead. Reduction of employment in the U.S. and increase of employment in China. Reduction of subsistence in the U.S. and increase of subsistence in China.

Theoretically speaking, the U.S. needs to send out workers together when relocating factories out from the U.S.

C) A majority or sheer number counts in case of democracy.

Manage both inequalities and monopolies.

It is not economically healthy to create small number of winners such as monopolies. We need to create new systems where the great body of people become winners because we have to live together peacefully without material richness. For this purpose, we have to reasonably reduce competition and sacrifice efficiency somewhat. This means that I am proposing conditional free economy conjunction with conditional democracy. Conditional acts like a brake for slowing down or stopping. Yes, I am proposing to gradually stop the engine of economy which is consumption driven engine.

Important point here is "gradually." Adam Smith always recommends gradual changes or shift instead of sudden or abrupt changes.

Economy will get stagnant without an engine but that is my whole point in this case. We are clearly seeing walls or limitations ahead of us when driving our car, for example, and thus we have to step on a brake pedal on necessary basis. Looking back to our history, it is not so bad being economically poor or scarce since we have only enjoyed economic abundance in the past 60 years or so after the WWII. As far as I know, our ancestors left Africa, exodus, about 50,000 years ago and migrated all over the world like now. In other words, at least we have 50,000 years of human history and we human beings had been economically poor for about 49,940 years. We have been economically poor for over 99.9% of the time in our history. Economy is not the only factor in our lives. We can enjoy arts without spending much money, for example. We can play guitars, sing songs, draw paintings, go hiking, go swimming, and go climbing without spending much money. Actually in Edo Era from 1600 to around 1900 when Japan closed door and Japanese lived like pretty much self-sufficient, we developed unique arts such as Kabuki, Ukiyo-e, and Haiku which still survives right now in Japan. It will not be so bad. Amish people in the U.S. are living pretty much self-sufficiently without even using electricity as far as I know.

Besides, as far as I read and learned, money, material wealth, being rich has a little contribution to our happiness on the condition that our basic needs are satisfied or met. This can also be explained by Abraham Maslow's' Hierarchy of Human needs theory. Most likely material wealth or being rich belongs to self-esteem which is lower needs than self-actualization needs. Also considering evolutionary theory, human beings have intrinsic animal nature deep inside of us as genes. When this animal nature, preservation of species, for example, including basic needs such as foods, shelters, clothes are satisfied, we human beings tend to aspire for higher/ different needs or wants which are self-actualization needs at the highest. In other words, we will not blindly look for more money nor more material wealth once we achieved to a certain level of wealth. Material wealth or economic prosperity needs to be reasonably satisfied but satisfactory level is good enough. Therefore, economic prosperity is not everything for us, although it is important part of it until it is satisfied up to a reasonable level.

Taking a look at Gini Statistics in the U.S., what we are doing is not satisfactory. Condition of Gini Statistics in getting worse in the U.S. these days. It means that fewer number of people got richer and larger number of people got poorer. We are making our situations worse off with respect to our happiness. Rich people will not get happier by getting richer anymore. Poor people will get less happy when their basic needs are threatened or infringed. Why is this happening? Monopolies or concentration of wealth, right?

We have to stop this trend right now. How? We have to change our whole systems including everything. In other words, we need to change rules of the game altogether. This is like moving from a fantasy land to an isolated island where we have to survive and live on self-sufficiently, for example. We can only spend what we produce here on an isolated island. If we change or shift our mindsets, we can say as follows:

<From an economic game to a survival game.>

We got bored about all you can eat and all you can drink competition.

Now we are starting a new game which is a survival game. We have to make our ends meet. This will be a game of management or survival. This is nothing new because we are doing it every day at both work and home.

Taking an example of hotel, we do not have to stay at the most expensive hotels and instead a reasonable or decent hotel should be fine for us, I guess.

VI. Re-booting or re-starting our economy.
<Treatment of unhealthy current market conditions.>
In the past, re-booting tasks were often times taken care of by wars. Since we have to avoid wars by all means, another option will be re-booting our economy by ourselves as follows:
a) Handle monopolies. Clear up stagnant economic conditions because of un-wanted monopolies. When and only when that monopolies get harmful for the economy, we can conduct the followings which is basically the same as taking over a bankrupt company by government for saving it. A good example is the case of GM, General Motors in the U.S. However, in our case the Earth Government should do it as follows:
We have following three options:

a-1) Dissolve the monopolistic company into pieces.
a-2) Governmentalize the monopolistic company or De-privatize the monopolistic company
a-3) Privatize or go public again after dissolving it into a couple of companies.

a-1) Dissolve the monopolistic company into pieces.
This is opposite of de-regulations. After de-regulations, most of the times we have created un-wanted monopolies again. Using anti-monopoly laws by the Earth Government, we should be able to control un-fair monopoly power. If it is not possible for us to control/manage monopolies, we have an option of dissolve it into pieces by using the Earth Government.

a-2) Governmentalize the monopolistic company or De-privatize the monopolistic company
Even when monopoly is an ideal situation such as water supply, for example, we still need to watch out for un-fair monopoly power. This is the case such as MS where global standard of OS is ideal and convenient, for example. This is almost the same as supply of water and electricity which are lifelines for us. When we are unable to control it by anti-monopoly laws or when MS takes an advantage of monopolistic power and enforces us to do what we do not want to persistently, we have an option of governmentalizing it.

a-3) Privatize or go public again after dissolving it into a couple of companies.
When we think that it is better off to put it in a free competition environment again, we can release the monopolistic company after dissolving it into a few companies to avoid monopolies.

<Abandon growth model.>
Because of limited resources, current growth business models are unfit. We have to control growth. We may need to minimize growth or go for non-growth model such as CIRCULAR ECONOMY in a reasonable

time period. Unfortunately, we may have to use regulations and/or impose taxes as disincentives. We have to have a proper balance between economic prosperity and our survival needs in the end.

<Last word>
Happiness come from within. Regardless of the conditions and situations, we can make ourselves happy inwardly. Actually mind or our brain cannot differentiate between the real events and the mental images we create in our minds. In other words, we can fool ourselves in our brains pretty much not by 100%, though. We can create peace in our minds or in our brains and live peacefully without physical joy such as overspending, for example. It is very important for us to keep abundant mentality in this kind of situation. We can enjoy abundance mentally only without physically spending very much. We can practice this kind of mentality by meditation and live like monks or priests.
We may meditate in the morning. Chanting mantra for a couple of hours like monks or priests those who have been doing it from ancient times in Europe. We eat healthy foods. We may grow vegetables and grains on the nearby gardens. In the end, we will live in a mental fancy world which our minds can create. It is up to us whether we live happily or not. Yes, we will live happily no matter what!

<Methodology>
<At Individual level>
From intemperance to temperance.
From idle and indolent to thrift and industry.
Conduct Benjamin Franklin Campaign.
Let everybody read the autobiography of Benjamin Franklin and live by the principles.
- Temperance.
- Thrift.
- Industry.
We need to teach at least the above three mentioned at every school and every companies in the U.S.
From consumption driven economy to industry driven economy.

We will follow Benjamin Franklin's teachings and start rebuilding our country from the scratch again.

<At Company Level>
Follow Adam Smith's teachings.
Things should be gradual and natural instead of artificial or too technical such as M&A's and products of financial markets.
Natural means laissez faire. (On the condition that it does not hurt the public interests.)
I also took it literally "Natural."
Anything unnatural should be restricted such as follows:
- M&As. This is a way of unnatural growth which facilitates monopolies.
- Stock split. This is not a natural growth. This is a psychological trick for leading to a misperception or misjudgment and thus we do not need it. I know some companies have done stock split once in a while, let's say once in 5 years or so for aiming for misperception of stock prices in order to attain easy stock valuations.
- Fund Money. This is the same as monopolies. Fund Money exercises dominant power in financial markets right now. Financial markets are no longer healthy in my opinion.

<Change a definition or concept of company>
NEW: Company is not only for investors but also for the public.
"For the public" was added to incorporate Benjamin Franklin's teachings.
Investors should only be able to demand to the extent that it does not hurt the public interests.
Both investors and workers need to follow Benjamin Franklin's teachings such as follows:
- Temperance. It means that avoid too extremes based on my understanding. Do not demand too much. This is one of the reasons why we lost factory jobs to Asia, especially China.
Stay in natural or gradual. This is the teaching of Adam Smith.
If we combine the above two teachings, it will be as follows:

We should be satisfied with moderation and also any changes or growth should be moderate and gradual. These should be our ethics which everybody will follow. We will abandon the current cruel business model, which is too demanding and leads us to too aggressive targets.

President J.F. Kennedy once said, "Ask what you can do for your country."

I dare to ask you, sir and madam, what can you do for your country?

This is the best I can do for your country.
This is my pay back for my education in the U.S.
Thank you all.
Thank you also for bearing with my mundane solutions, clumsy English, lousy formatting, and disorganized and repetitive structure of this book.
I apologize for them.

Let us prevail!

September 2016.
Hiroshi Morita

Bibliography

Abraham H. Maslow, Maslow on Management, John Wiley & Sons, Inc., 1998.

Abraham H. Maslow, Motivation and Personality third edition, Addison Wesley Longman, 1954, 1987.

Adam Smith, "Books I-III Complete and Unabridged", The Wealth of Nations, Classic House, 2009.

Adam Smith, "Books IV-V", The Wealth of Nations, Penguin Classics, 1776, 1999.

Al Gore, The Future, Random House, 2013.

Al Gore, an inconvenient truth, Viking/Rodale2006, 2007.

Alexander Green, Beyond Wealth, Wiley, 2011.

Angus Maddison, Contours of The World Economy 1-2030 AD, Oxford, 2007.

Arnold Schwarzenegger, Total Recall, Simon & Schuster, 2012.

Benjamin Franklin, The Autobiography of Benjamin Franklin second edition, Yale University Press, 1964.

Bob Thomas, Walt Disney, Disney, 1976, 1994.

Brendon Burchard, The motivation Manifesto, Hay House, Inc., 2014.

Brian Tracy, Advanced Selling Strategies, Simon & Schuster Paperbacks, 1995.

Brian Tracy, Million Dollar Habits, Entrepreneur Press, 2006.

Burton Goldberg, Alternative Medicine, Future Medicine Publishing Inc.,

Byron Katie, Loving What Is, Three Rivers Press, 2002.

Charles T. Munger, Poor Charlie's Almanack expanded third edition, Donning, 2005.

Chase and Aquilano, Productions and Operations Management 4th edition, Irwin, 1985.

Chris Anderson, Makers, Crown Business, 2012.

Daniel G. Amen, M.D., The Amen Solution, Three Rivers Press, 2011.

Daniel G. Amen, M.D., Change Your Brain Change Your Life, Three Rivers Press, 1998.

David A. Aaker, Building Strong Brands, Free Press, 1996.

David A. Aaker and George S. Pay, Marketing Research 3rd edition, Wiley, 1980, 1983, 1986.

David Abodaher, Iacocca, Zebra Books, 1982.

David Halberstam, The Best And The Brightest, Penguin Books, 1969, 1971, 1972, 1983.

Deepak Chopra, M.D., Rudolph E. Tanzi, Ph.D., Super Brain, Harmony Books, 2012.

Deepak Chopra, M.D., The Book of Secrets, Thee Rivers Press, 2004.

Deepak Chopra, M.D., Perfect Health, Three Rivers Press, 1991, 2000.

Dr. Denis Waltley, The Psychology of Winning, Berkley Books, 1979.

Don Miguel Ruiz, The Four Agreements, Amber-Allen Publishing, 1997.

Eben Alexander, M.D., Proof of Heaven, Simon & Schuster Paperbacks, 2012.

Eckhart Tolle, The Power of Now, New World Library, 1999.

The Economics Problem Solver, REA, 1980, 1984.

The Economist, Mega Change The world in 2050, The Economist Newspaper Ltd, 2012.

Edgar K. Browning and Jacquelene M. Browning, Microeconomic theory and Applications 2nd edition, Little Brown, 1986.

Florence Scovel, The game of Life and How to Play it, DeVorss Publications, 1925.

Francia, Porter, and Strawser, Managerial Accounting 5th edition, Dame Publication Inc., 1984.

Francis J. Kelly & Heather Mayfield Kelly, What They Really Teach You at The Harvard Business School, Warner Books, 1986.

Gary L. Lilien and Philip Kotler, Marketing Decision Making, Harper & Row, 1983.

George Bush with Victor Gold, Looking Forward, Bantam Books, 1987.

George Colombo, Capturing Customers.com, Career Press, 2001.

Glen L. Urban and John R. Hauser, Design and Marketing of New Products, Prentice Hall, 1980.

Hale Dwoskin and Lester Levenson, Happiness is Free, Sedona, 2002.

Heinz Weihrich, Management Excellence, McGraw-Hill, 1986, 1987.

Hiroshi Morita, "A Comparison Study of Distribution Systems between the United States and Japan", thesis, University of California, Riverside, August 1987.

Jack Canfield, The Success Principles, Collins, 2005.

James Allen, As a Man Thinkth, Tribeca Books, 1910.

James Arthur Ray, The Science of Success, Sunark Press, 2006.

James F. Engel, Roger D. Blackwell, and Paul W. Miniard, Consumer Behavior 5th edition, 1968, 1973, 1978, 1982, 1986.

James C. Van Horne, Financial Management and Policy 7th edition, Prentice Hall, 1968, 1971, 1974, 1977, 1980, 1983, 1986.

James P. Quirk, Intermediate Microeconomics second edition, SRA, 1982, 1976.

Janet Bray Attwood and Chris Attwood, Your Hidden Riches, Harmony Books, 2014.

Jay Abraham, Getting Everything You Can out of All You've Got, Truman Talley Books, 2000.

Jay Conrad Levinson, Guerrilla Marketing, Houghton Mifflin, 2007.

Jen Sincero, You are a Badass, Rienneng Press, 2013.

Jerry Porras, Stewart Emery, and Mark Thompson, Success Built to Last, A Plume Book, 2007.

Jim Collins, Good to Great, Collins Business, 2001.

J. Krishnamurti, The Book of Life, Harper One, 1995.

Joe Girard, How to Sell Anything to Anybody, A Fireside Book, 1977, 2005.

John Kao, Entrepreneurship, Creativity, & Organization, Prentice-Hall, 1989.

Jonathan Haidt, The Happiness Hypothesis, Basic Books, 2006.

Joseph Murphy, The Miracle of Mind Dynamics, Prentice Hall, 1964.

Joseph Murphy, The Power of Your Subconscious Mind, Wilder Publications, 2007.

Joseph Murphy, Think Yourself to Health, Wealth & Happiness, Prentice Hall, 2002.

Josh Ozersky, Colonel Sanders, University of Texas Press, 2012.

Kenichi Ohmae, The Mind of The Strategist, Penguin Books, 1983, 1985, 1986, 1987.

Kenneth Primozic, Edward Primozic, and Joe Leben, Strategic Choices, McGraw Hill, 1991.

Lee Iacocca, Talking Straight, Bantam Books, 1988.

Louis W. Stern and Adel I. El-Ansary, Marketing Channels 4th edition, Prentice=Hall, 1992.

Laurence C Smith, The World in 2050, Plume, 2011.

Lester R. Brown, The Great Transition, W. W. Norton, 2015.

Lincoln L. Chao, Statistics for Management 2nd edition, The Sciebtific Press, 1980, 1984.

Makridakis, Wheelwright, and McGEE, Forecasting, Wiley, 1978, 1983.

Manoj Singh, "The 2007-08 Financial Crisis in Review", October 28, 2008.

Marsha Sinetar, To Build the Life You Want, Create the Work You Love, St. Martin Griffin, 1995.

Martin E.P. Seligman, Ph.D., Authentic Happiness, ATRIA, 2002.

Michael S. Gazzaniga, Todd F. Heatherton, Diane F. Halpern, Psychological Science third edition, W. W. Norton & Company, 2010, 2006, 2003.

Michael E. Gerber, Awakening the Entrepreneur Within, Collins, 2008.

Michael O'Connor, Ted Turner, Greenwood Press, 2010.

Milton Friedman, Bright Promises, Dismal Performance, Harcourt Brace Jovanovich, 1972, 1975, 1983.

Napoleon Hill, Law of Success, Highroads Media Inc., 2003.

Napoleon Hill and W. Clement Stone, Success through a Positive Mental Attitude, Pocket Books, 1960, 1977, 1987.

Norman Vincent Peale, The Power of Positive Thinking, Exciting Classics, 2013.

Otto Kleppner, Advertising Procedure 9th edition, Prentice-Hall, 1925, 1933, 1941, 1950, 1966, 1973, 1979, 1983, 1986.

Peter F. Drucker, The Practice of Management, Perennial Library, 1982.

Philip Kotler, Marketing Management 6th edition, Prentice Hall, 1967, 1972, 1976, 1980, 1984, 1988.

Ray Kroc, Grinding it out, St. Martin's Paperbacks, 1977.

Robert Kiyosaki, Cashflow Quadrant, Warner Business Books, 1998, 1999.

Robert Kiyosaki, Rich Dad Poor Dad, Warner Business Books, 1997, 1998.

Richard Bandler, Get The Life You Want, Health Communications, Inc., 2008.

Richard Branson, Losing my Virginity, Crown Business, 1998, 2002, 2005, 2007.

Richard Brealey and Stewart Myers, Principles of Corporate Finance 2nd edition, McGraw Hill, 1981, 1984.

Richard Dawkins, The Extended Phenotype, Oxford, 1982, 1999.

Richard Dawkins, The Greatest Show on Earth, Free Press, 2009.

Richard Dawkins, The Magic of Reality, Free Press, 2011.

Richard Dawkins, The Selfish Gene 30th anniversary edition, Oxford, 1976, 1989, 2006.

Robert G. Allen, Creating Wealth, Free Press, 1983, 1986, 2006.

Robert D. Auerbach, Money, Banking, and Financial Markets 2nd edition, Macmillan Publishing Company, 1985.

Robert J. Barro, Macroeconomics, John Wiley & Son, 1984.

Robert Bruce Bowin, Human Resource Problem Solving, Prentice-Hall, 1987.

Robert B. Cialdini, Ph.D., Influence, Collins Business, 1984, 1994, 2007.

Robert J. Ringer, Million Dollar Habits, Fauceit Crest, 1990.

Sam Walton, Made in America, Bantam Books, 1993.

Scot, Martin, Petty, Keown, Basic Financial Management 4th edition, Prentice-Hall, 1979, 1982, 1985, 1988.

Stephen R. Covey, The 7 Habits of Highly Effective People, A Fireside Book, 1989.

Tal Ben-Shahar, Ph.D., Happier, Mc Graw Hill, 2007.

Thomas J. Peters & Robert H. Waterman, Jr., In Search of Excellence, Warner Books, 1982.

Thomas J. Stanley, Ph.D. and William D. Danko, Ph.D., The Millionaire Next Door, Pocket Books, 1996.

Tina Seeling, inGenius, Harper Collins, 2011.

Tom Peters, Liberation Management, Knopf, 1992.

Tom Peters, Thriving on Chaos, Harper Perennial, 1987.

Tony Dungy, Quiet Strength, Tyndale Momentum, 2007.

Tony Hsieh, Delivering Happiness, Business Plus, 2010.

Tony Schwarts, The Way We're Working isn't Working, Free Press, 2010.

Wallace D. Wattles, The Science of Getting Rich, SoHo Books, 2012.

Ward Hanson, Principles of Internet Marketing, South-Western College Publishing, 2000.

Warren J. Keegan, Multinational Marketing Management 3rd edition, Prentice-Hall, 1974, 1980, 1984.

William Clement Stone, The Success System That Never Fails, BN Publishing, 2010.

Zev Chafets, Remembering Who We Are, Penguin, 2015.

Data Source:

Bureaus of Economic Analysis.

BEA US International Trade.

Bureau of labor statistics.

FRB S.T. Louis.

Indexmundi.com.

Statista.com.

Tradingeconomics.com.

Treasurydirect.

US Census Bureau.

Treasury.gov.

Wiki.

World Bank.

About the Author:

Hiroshi Morita.

In the U.S., he received his MBA major in marketing from UCR, University of California Riverside in 1987.

In Japan, he received his bachelor degree in commercial science from Waseda University in Tokyo in 1982.

He worked several international companies in Japan mainly in the field of product management. He managed a couple of brands successfully but he suffered from stress-related illness and thus he just quit. He realized that this is a rat race according to Mr. Robert Kiyosaki's expression and thus it is not worth it in his opinion. Since then he has been living in Tokyo very quietly while managing his internet shop. As he felt danger intrinsically, now he woke up and he has something to say to the whole world before it is too late.

www.ingramcontent.com/pod-product-compliance
Lightning Source LLC
Chambersburg PA
CBHW080655190526
45169CB00006B/2126